W9-CES-842

Leaders of Transition

Also by Martin Westlake

BRITAIN'S EMERGING EURO-ELITE? The British in the European Parliament 1979–1992

THE COMMISSION AND THE PARLIAMENT: Partners and Rivals in the European Policymaking Process

A MODERN GUIDE TO THE EUROPEAN PARLIAMENT

BRITISH POLITICS AND EUROPEAN ELECTIONS 1994 (*with David Butler*)

BRITISH POLITICS AND EUROPEAN ELECTIONS 1999 (*forthcoming, with David Butler*)

THE COUNCIL OF THE EUROPEAN UNION

THE EUROPEAN UNION BEYOND AMSTERDAM: New Concepts of European Integration (*editor*)

Leaders of Transition

Edited by
Martin Westlake

First published in Great Britain 2000 by
MACMILLAN PRESS LTD
Houndmills, Basingstoke, Hampshire RG21 6XS and London
Companies and representatives throughout the world

A catalogue record for this book is available from the British Library.

ISBN 0–333–73394–0

 First published in the United States of America 2000 by
ST. MARTIN'S PRESS, INC.,
Scholarly and Reference Division,
175 Fifth Avenue, New York, N.Y. 10010

ISBN 0–312–22867–8

Library of Congress Cataloging-in-Publication Data
Leaders of transition / edited by Martin Westlake.
p.   cm.
Includes bibliographical references and index.
ISBN 0–312–22867–8 (cloth)
1. Political leadership—Case studies.   2. Political development—Case studies.   I.
Westlake, Martin.

JC330.3.L395   1999
909.82'5'0922 21—dc21   99–045012

This book is printed on paper suitable for recycling and made from fully managed and sustained
forest sources.

10   9   8   7   6   5   4   3   2   1
09   08   07   06   05   04   03   02   01   00

Printed and bound in Great Britain by
Antony Rowe Ltd, Chippenham, Wiltshire

To **Oliver**
a veritable leader of transition

Contents

List of Illustrations

Acknowledgements

Leaders of Transition is the first in a projected series of studies of like phenomena which stretch across political systems and historical periods. Other titles in the series will include *Political Survivors, Political Dynasties, Powers behind Thrones* and *Benevolent Dictators?* I owe a great debt of thanks to my commissioning editor at Macmillan, Tim Farmiloe, for his enthusiasm and encouragement, and indeed for taking on such an apparently eclectic series of titles. Having read and edited all the contributions to this volume, I believe his faith has been rewarded. Each of the case studies is fascinating in its own right; together they reveal a great deal about the nature of political behaviour in particular but recurring circumstances.

Each of the contributors to this volume is owed special thanks. Archie Brown cheerfully agreed to pen a chapter when this volume was little more than a twinkle in its editor's eye. Despite mushrooming commitments he stuck loyally to the project and has provided a fascinating account of the achievements of a man who is undoubtedly one of the twentieth century's major figures. Martin Bull delivered an authoritative analysis despite his heavy duties as head of the Political Science Department at Salford University and the arrival of his son, Anthony Martin. John Fitzmaurice provided considerable help in bringing the project to fruition. It was he who suggested the cases of Jaruzelski and Suarez, and as always he acted as an extremely fertile sounding board. Simon Parlier ably stepped into the breach and provided an authoritative chapter on Adolfo Suarez. Many ideas were exchanged during a shared holiday in the Basque country, where much of the manuscript was edited, and his chapter-in-progress provided an excellent excuse for enjoyable excursions to the bookshops of Bilbao, Pamplona and San Sebastian. David Welsh and Jack Spence were kind enough to join the project at a very early stage and the resulting chapter on F. W. de Klerk gives an impressive account of another major political figure of the twentieth century (and, like Gorbachev, a winner of the Nobel Peace Prize). All the contributors were generous with their time, rereading various parts of the manuscript and offering much helpful and constructive criticism.

I would also like to thank Ian St John and Jo and Derek Owen for reading and commenting on various parts of the manuscripts.

Marie and Cengiz Seren, John Williams and Simon Parlier were very helpful in tracking down photographs, and I would like to put on record my thanks to the European Pressphoto Agency for permission to reproduce the photographs on pages 1 and 27. Thanks go also to Giorgio Forattini for permission to publish the cartoon on page 64.

Alison Howson at Macmillan shepherded the manuscript ably through the trials and tribulations of the production process, and Keith Povey copy-edited the manuscript with customary skill and tact.

A special vote of thanks goes to my family for their patience, support and indulgence; to Godelieve, Emily and Oliver. This book is dedicated to Oliver, who arrived in mid-project but who, like long-suffering Emily before him, obligingly decided to take long afternoon naps at weekends and in many other ways tolerantly enabled his father to bring the project to fruition.

MARTIN WESTLAKE

Notes on the Contributors

Archie Brown is Professor of Politics at the University of Oxford, a Fellow of St Antony's College and author of *The Gorbachev Factor*.

Martin Bull is Professor of Italian Politics and Head of Department at Salford University.

John Fitzmaurice is Professor of European Politics at the Free University of Brussels and will shortly be publishing *Politics and Government in Central Europe*.

Simon Parlier is Senior Editor at Encyclopaedias Bordas, Paris.

Jack Spence is Former Director of Studies and Associate Fellow of the Royal Institute of International Affairs.

David Welsh is Professor Emeritus of Politics at Cape Town University, South Africa.

Martin Westlake is Professor of European Politics at the College of Europe, Bruges, is Associate Member of the Centre for Legislative Studies at the University of Hull, and is currently writing a biography of Neil Kinnock.

Wither is fled the visionary gleam?
Where is it now, the glory and the dream?

(Wordsworth, ***Intimations of Mortality***)

Introduction: Leaders or Led?

Martin Westlake

And when we think we lead, we are most led (Byron, The Two Foscari)

The late François Mitterrand once likened political leadership to the act of riding a tiger; despite the outward impression of control, leaders spend much of their time trying to hang on to the tiger of history, as events mostly beyond their control lope inexorably onwards. This book had its origins in the observation of an apparently simple phenomenon. Sometimes the political process throws up leaders who identify a need for radical change, use their position of power to bring about that change, but thereafter seem unable to benefit from the change themselves. I was certainly not alone in having noticed this phenomenon (see for example Parris, 1997), but I wanted to explore it further. What motivates these leaders of transition? Are they really responsible for the conscious release of forces for change, or are they, in line with Mitterrand's world-weary observation, simply bowing before a series of inevitabilities? If they genuinely do bring about change, what is their reason? Are their acts inspired by reference to higher prescriptive values (loyalty for example, or patriotism), or by baser desires to stay in control and hence in power? If they do trigger change in order to stay in control, does their chosen strategy work? If on the contrary they trigger change for some altruistic reason, is their role recognised and is it rewarded?

This volume brings together case studies of six political leaders who seem, at first sight at least, to provide examples of the phenomenon of the leader of transition as described above: Mikhail Gorbachev, Adolfo Suárez, F. W. de Klerk, General Wojciech Jaruzelski, Achille Occhetto and Neil Kinnock. Each led his party or his country. Each enacted a process of change on the basis of his position and his personal authority. Each seemed to have enacted a transition which, in the greater scheme of things, was seen as being for the better. Yet each seemed unable to benefit from the change he had brought about, or to put another way, none of these leaders were able to draw any advantage from the change they enacted. Why, then, did they do it? What motivated them to seek the kinds of transition that they – at the least – initiated? Was it simple self-preservation, a desire for advancement or, for those already at the summit of power, to maintain their incumbency, or was it perhaps done with reference to some ulterior moral value? Were there parallels or similarities between these experiences?

Mikhail Gorbachev became general secretary of the Soviet Communist Party in 1985, when, as Archie Brown reminds us in Chapter 1, 'both the division of Europe and the continuation of the Cold War were simply taken for granted'. He had been described as a 'prophet without honour in his own country':

> The man who ended Soviet totalitarianism, arranged for free elections, a free press, freedom of worship, new legislatures and a multi-party system: the man who introduced a pluralistic economy and opened Soviet Union to the world outside; the man who almost single-handedly ended the Cold War and the arms race; who invented glasnost and perestroika ... is consigned by his own and the succeeding generation to a drab ante-room near the entrance to a new world (Parris, 1997).

Adolfo Suárez seemed to be a classic Spanish careerist technocrat, rising up through the ranks of General Franco's authoritarian political system. But King Juan Carlos had spotted something in the man. An almost anonymous figure, Suárez was appointed Spanish prime minister in 1976 to widespread critical reaction in both the reformist and the reactionary camps, but thereafter almost immediately set about dismantling the system that had produced him with 'skill, nerve, generosity and astounding decisiveness (ibid.) He moved rapidly and deftly to legalise all political parties, including the Communist Party, and the trades unions. A year later he won Spain's first democratic elections, but proved less adept at leading a party and faltered. He was replaced and later enobled and is now largely forgotten outside his own country, where the young and charismatic Felipe González came to personify Spain's transition to democracy. As Parlier points out in Chapter 6, here, surely was a leader of transition *par excellence*, bringing Spain from the dying days of the Francoist regime into the family of modern Western European democratic states.

F. W. de Klerk was the scion of a highly political Afrikaner nationalist family. A gifted lawyer, he rapidly became involved in National Party politics, with a firm commitment to apartheid, and entered the national parliament in 1972. A rising star, he became a cabinet member in 1978 and thereafter held a succession of ministerial portfolios, ultimately becoming state president in 1989. He had to contend with a potential haemorrhage of support to the breakaway Conservative Party, and this led him to adopt an increasingly reactionary stance. Inwardly, however, de Klerk was preparing for change. As Welsh and Spence point out in Chapter 2, his 2 February 1990 speech to the Cape town parliament, in which he announced the release of Nelson Mandela and lifted the ban on the African National Congress, effectively heralded the end of nearly 350 years of white rule in South Africa. Thereafter he was central to the negotiated and largely peaceful transition process. As Welsh and Spence underline, it was 'a rare political feat for a minority to yield power to a majority that was, moreover, racially and culturally alien'. The achievement won him and Nelson Mandela the Nobel Prize, but de Klerk's political career ended awkwardly, in allegations and counterallegations about the exact relationship of the Nationalist Party government to the state-sponsored violence which increasingly scarred the apartheid state and how much de Klerk personally knew.

General Wojciech Jaruzelski was a career soldier with a strong Catholic upbringing. His formative years were spent in Russia. He took part in the liberation of Poland and was part of the nucleus of the new army of communist Poland. Thereafter he rose through the ranks, becoming an apparently orthodox (and reactionary) member of the PZPR (Communist Party) leadership. This orthodoxy led him to support hard-line action – including complicity in the ordering of troops to fire on anticommunist demonstrators in Gdansk in 1970 – and, once appointed prime minister in 1981, to the imposition of martial law and the outlawing of Solidarnosc. Yet some eight years later this self-same Jaruzelski launched a round table of talks with Solidarnosc which led directly to elections, triggering Poland's transition to full democracy. Despite this, Jaruzelski is remembered as a sinister and villified figure whose motives, as Fitzmaurice points out in Chapter 4, remain fundamentally ambiguous.

Achille Occhetto was a Turin-born, middle-class boy with a typical Catholic unbringing who subsequently entered the Italian Communist Party (PCI) as a teenager and displayed early political promise, becoming leader of the party's youth movement. He was later appointed as a regional party leader in Sicily and elected to the Chamber of Deputies in 1976. Although initially considered to be on the left of the party, he subsequently became a centrist and a loyal party man, supporting Berlinguer's 1973 'Historic Compromise' strategy and becoming right-hand man to the new leader, Natta, after Berlinguer's untimely death. He was himself almost unanimously elected to the party leadership in 1988. Five days after the collapse of the Berlin Wall in October 1989, Occhetto announced his intention to dissolve the PCI and found a new, non-communist party of the left. This was seen by most Italians, communists and non-communists alike, as an extraordinarily sudden and revolutionary initiative.

As Martin Bull recounts in Chapter 3, within two years the new Democratic Party of the Left (PDS) had been created. Italy's 'communist question' was no longer an issue, the party system had been unblocked, and in April 1996 a centre-left coalition, with the PDS as its principal component, won the general election and governed Italy until October 1998. But in the meantime Occhetto himself had been ignominiously removed from the leadership and exiled to the political sidelines of the European Parliament.

Neil Kinnock was born into a mining family in a South Wales valley, in Aneurin Bevan's constituency. His was a pure, working-class, Labour pedigree. Kinnock showed an early interest in politics and was active as a student, becoming president of the Cardiff University Students' Union. A series of fortuitous circumstances, combined with extraordinary oratory and innate political skills, saw him elected to the Commons at the youthful age of 28 and elected leader of the opposition at the age of 40. Kinnock's elevation to the leadership owed much to the widespread perception that he would be a moderniser able to pull Labour back from the brink of the abyss, but he was also seen as a man of the left, supporting, among other things, withdrawal from the EC and unilateral disarmament. Over the next eight years and through two general elections Kinnock transformed the Labour Party from an increasingly marginalised and anarchic party on the brink of electoral collapse to a modern social-democratic party. These reforms ultimately bore fruit in the 1994 Euro-elections and, most strikingly, in the 1997 general election. But as the 1992 general election demonstrated, Kinnock's left-wing origins and the changes he had brought about combined to disqualify him from the ultimate prize of electoral success and the leadership of his country. As I point out in Chapter 5, he was brought down by a paradox: either he had changed his principles, in which case his enemies could argue that this was electoral opportunism, or the change was only superficial, in which case his opponents could frighten voters with the prospect that he might return to the left once in power. Today the veracity of the transition he wrought is no longer disputed:

> We gasp at the achievements of Tony Blair, who came rather late to courage. We salute the memory of John Smith, who proved timid but was redeemed by death. But at the record of the man who kicked over the Militant tables and wrenched his party away from the past, we only snigger. Tony Blair is not the originator of new Labour; he is the product of it. Mr Kinnock was seen by the socialist companions of his youth as selling out on socialism; and among Labour's rootless young newcomers it is not fashionable to acknowledge the bravery of those who were brave when to be brave you did have to be brave. Mr Kinnock's reputation is therefore lost in a limbo between old Labour and new. But it was he who ushered in the new (Parris, 1997).

In each of these cases, alternative and equally plausible strategies and options seemed to have been available. As Brown points out in Chapter 1, Gorbachev was under no immediate pressure to introduce potentially far-reaching and problematic reforms and could just as easily have chosen the more cautious and secure option of presiding over the gradual decline of the Soviet Union. Although King Juan Carlos had somehow seen that Adolfo Suárez might become an agent of change, in Chapter 6 Parlier recalls how the combined pressure of the Francoist camp, the army and the church could just as easily have intimidated Suarez into opting for inertia and a more repressive version of the *status quo*. In the case of South Africa, international sanctions were clearly biting and in Chaper 2 Welsh and Spence describe how de Klerk had sensed for some years that the political system was under threat. Morever P. W. Botha had laid rudimentary foundations for a transitional strategy of some sort. But as a reactionary figure, seen as being on the right of his party, de Klerk might just as easily have opted for a more intransigent stance, with recourse to more, rather than less, repressive policies. As Fitzmaurice underlines in Chapter 4, Jaruzelski was similarly confronted with another, perhaps more natural option, especially given his previous track record of hard-line policies and the imposition of martial law. Like his neighbour, Erich Honecker, Jaruzelski (a military man, after all) could have opted for an authoritarian approach rather than the Magdalenka process.

Gorbachev's reforms and the sudden collapse of the Soviet system were evidently key elements in relation to several of these transitions. It was, write Welsh and Spence, the Soviet transformation which drew the sting of the 'communist menace' in relation to the ANC in South Africa, and it was Gorbachev's implicit acquiescence which enabled Jaruzelski to contemplate the round table option in Poland in 1988–89 (the two men got on well). Similarly the collapse of the USSR effectively undermined the 'Marchais option' (that is, of clinging to power, remaining hardline and of overseeing the consequent electoral decline) for Achille Occhetto. Nevertheless he could have followed a more orthodox strategy which would have left him in firm command of a much-reduced but more coherent PCI (as indeed the breakaway Refounded Communism Party has become – and ironically this might still have guaranteed Occhetto a slice of the governmental cake). Kinnock faced a similar choice between a politically more natural policy stance (which would have rendered Labour increasingly irrelevant to the electorate) and the more pragmatic process of policy reform which he once described as 'socialism by plod'.

But to what extent did these leaders *really* have a choice? Like all politicians, they were interactive, responding to their surrounding environment. At any one moment they would presumably have identified the range of options open to them, and assessed the likely consequences of each. Changes to their political environment, particularly once the transition process had been initiated, could just as easily have limited the range of their options. This observation brings us back to the tiger metaphor of François Mitterrand (who after all could himself be described as a leader of transition on a par with Achille Occhetto and Neil Kinnock). Did these leaders manipulate their political environment, or were they manipulated by it? The question was put to each of the contributors. Were these leaders of transition constrained to act in the way they did, both initially and as the transition process continued, and if so to what extent? The answer to this question immediately gives rise to another. If these leaders were not fundamentally constrained, why did they do it?

The question arises as to how these particular leaders of transition were selected for this study. At the methodological level I might be accused of loading the dice by choosing as case studies only those leaders of transition who corresponded to the profile I initially had in mind. What about other leaders of transition whose actions were, in ethical terms, not as commendable (for example Richard Nixon or Deng Xiaoping), or who survived the transition process (for example

Kemal Atatürk, Charles de Gaulle, Willy Brandt, Mario Soares or Vaclav Havel)? What about leaders of *partial* transition or, as currently exist in many South-East Asian countries, leaders of economic transition alone? If the choice of leaders considered in this volume was not random, on what basis was it made?

The simple answer is that this book does not address the overall phenomenon of the leadership of transition but rather a very particular subset within it: those who, as described at the outset, seemed unable to benefit from the change they brought about. There is something humanly and intellectually interesting in such a phenomenon. In addition, it is at least potentially paradoxical. If these leaders knew that they would not be able to benefit from the changes they initiated, then we are confronted with the very rare phenomenon of political altruism. If we exclude misjudgement or mistakenness, they must logically have initiated change for the benefit of somebody or something. At the other extreme, if they did expect to benefit, the simple truth is that they were unable to do so, and so hubris and a tragic element must enter the analysis.

There is a long tradition of studying leadership. The bookshelves groan under the weight of books about military leadership and leadership in business. Political philosophers from Macchiavelli to Gramsci to Weber have grappled with the concept of the good or the effective leader. No self-respecting modern political study is complete without consideration of the role of the democratically elected leadership and the strategies which elections impose. Political biographies – whether of democratic or non-democratic leaders – abound (for example Alistair Cole's 1997 biography of Mitterrand is essentially a study of political leadership in France). An American literature has developed on the psychology of political leadership and on the evolutionary motivation for leadership (see for example Gardner, 1996; Sulloway, 1996), and there have been recent moves towards developing the comparative study of executive political leadership in the West (see for example Blondel and Thiébault, 1991). Moreover there is a large literature on transitions to democracy, embracing the study of the role of leaders and other individuals, and a similarly extensive literature on political leadership in communist countries.

This study contributes to three different areas of the literature: that on political leadership in communist systems; that on political leadership in liberal democracies; and that on transitions to democracy from authoritarian rule. But I would argue that it also goes beyond these areas and is distinct from them, because it focuses specifically on political leadership during periods of considerable change, change at least partly initiated by those leaders themselves. Because the primary focus is change, the study is able to consider and compare leadership in both authoritarian regimes and liberal democracies, something which, with a few exceptions, the literature has not done to date.

There are, I believe, understandable reasons for this lack of comparative study. At a normative level, such studies would have had to encompass both democratic and non-democratic leadership. We were perhaps uncomfortable at the implication that the two might share qualities, particularly during the extended period of the Cold War. But even in this normative context there is no *a priori* reason why a democratic leader should necessarily be morally good, nor why a non-democratic leader should necessarily be bad (indeed it is my intention to explore the phenomenon of the 'benevolent dictator' in a later volume in this series). Certainly we know that some democratic leaders have displayed bad moral qualities, whilst some non-democratic leaders have done good.

At the analytical level, the literature has also suffered from compartmentalisation. Thus the literature on communist regimes concentrates solely on communist regime leadership, which by its nature is more likely to constrain change than to promote it. The literature on leadership in Western liberal democracies deals only with the West and tends to focus on leadership stability and the transmission of power rather than change, and, with the literature on communist regimes, certainly not systemic change. On the other hand the literature on transition from authoritarian rule to democracy *does* concentrate on change, but it tends not to focus on individuals and is very much limited by its own paradigm. It is concerned with analysing leadership, together with many other possible contributory factors, *only* of regimes undergoing transition. This study is concerned with the broader phenomenon of political transition, in both 'East' and 'West', and of individual leaders' roles within it. I would therefore modestly claim that this study is distinctive. It draws on and contributes to the literature but at the some time it establishes its own niche.

If I may anticipate the concluding chapter a little, it is reassuring to know that, in a century which has spawned such opportunistic tyrants as Hitler, Stalin, Mao and Pol Pot, there are politicians – truly ethical beings, as I shall argue – who are able to step outside the systems which nurtured them and consider the wider good. Whilst I would not pretend that this investigation has unearthed any deep theoretical truths, these fascinating case studies do vindicate my initial belief that here was a generalised phenomenon which, as well as being of great human interest, was worthy of academic study. I believe it demonstrates how it is both possible and worthwhile to compare political phenomena across communist, post-communist and liberal-democratic regimes.

References

Blondel, Jean and Jean-Louis Thiébault (eds) (1991), *The Profession of Government Minister in Western Europe*, London: Macmillan.

Cole, Alistair (1997) *François Mitterrand: A Study in Leadership* (London: Routledge).

Gardner, Howard in collaboration with Emma Laskin (1996), *Leading Minds: An Anatomy of Leadership* (London: HarperCollins).

Gramsci, Antonio (1978), *The Modern Prince and Other Writings* (New York: International Publishers).

Machiavelli, Niccolo (1952) *The Prince* (London: New English Library).

Naughton, John (1996) 'Too many chiefs?', *Observer*, 7 January.

Parris, Matthew (1997) 'Heroes of transition', *The Times*, 7 March.

Sulloway, Frank (1996) *Born to Rebel* (Boston, Mass.: Little, Brown).

Tyler, Christian (1996) 'The search for the makings of greatness', *Financial Times*, 2–3 November.

Weber, Max (1948) 'Politics as a Vocation', in H. Gerth and C. Wright Mills (eds), *From Max Weber: Essays in Sociology* (London: Routledge and Kegan Paul).

Mikhail Gorbachev

He was a genetic error of the system
(Andrei Grachev, 1991)

Boris Yeltsin gazes towards the political future Mikhail Gorbachev's reforms
have effectively created for him. (*Courtesy of the European Pressphoto Agency*)

1
Mikhail Gorbachev: Systemic Transformer

Archie Brown

He was a genetic error of the system (Andrei Grachev, 1991)[1]

Argument will long continue about exactly how great was Mikhail Gorbachev's role in changing the Soviet Union, but no one can doubt the extent of the change. The state moved from having 'elections' with only one candidate's name on the ballot paper to contested elections; from a rubber-stamp, pseudo-parliament to an argumentative legislature with real powers; from a totally state-owned and state-controlled economy to the beginnings of a mixed economy and a market; from strict censorship to freedom of expression and publication; from closed borders to freedom of travel; and from religious persecution to religious tolerance – in short, from extreme authoritarianism to political pluralism. Ultimately, both the communist system and the Soviet state were transformed out of existence. In the space formerly occupied by the USSR there are now fifteen successor states, of which one, Russia, remains the largest country on Earth.

That those fundamental changes took place within less than seven years without war or revolution is remarkable enough. Of at least as great importance as these internal developments both for Russia and for the outside world was the transformation which occurred simultaneously in international relations. It had long been assumed that the Soviet rulers saw the client communist regimes of Eastern Europe as no more than their country's due reward for contributing more than any other state to the defeat in Europe of Hitler's Germany. There was, indeed, plenty of evidence to indicate that the Soviet leadership, military and security forces viewed their hegemony over Eastern Europe as non-negotiable. Soviet invasion had crushed the Hungarian Revolution of 1956 and had ended the Prague Spring in 1968. In

Poland fear of such direct military intervention was a major factor inducing General Vojciech Jaruzelski to crack down on the independent trade union and political movement, Solidarity, in 1981.

In Washington and other Western capitals, as recently as 1985 when Gorbachev became Soviet leader, both the division of Europe and the continuation of the Cold War were simply taken for granted. At a conference I attended in February 1985 of politicians, senior officials, academics and journalists from Britain and the United States to discuss East–West relations, a former British ambassador, in his summing-up, spoke for the overwhelming majority (though not quite 'all') when he said: 'There's one thing we all know. The Soviet Union isn't going to change.' One month later the Central Committee of the Communist Party of the Soviet Union unanimously elected Mikhail Gorbachev to its general secretaryship. In fairness, it should be added that the Soviet selectorate, too, did not know that they were choosing someone who would pursue far-reaching reform, still less shake the system to its foundations. One of those who attended the decisive Politburo meeting, Vladimir Dolgikh, then a secretary of the Central Committee and a candidate member of the Politburo, admitted later that he did not at that time 'have a clue' that Gorbachev would engage in sweeping change of the Soviet system (Roxburgh, 1991, p. 9). Others have said much the same thing.

In East-Central Europe the hopes for change, while not non-existent, were exceedingly modest. In the words of Rita Klímová, a friend of Václav Havel and the first post-communist ambassador of Czechoslovakia (as it then was) to the United States: 'The most we could hope for was that we'd be able to go as far as Hungary.'[2] What she had in mind was the reforms introduced under János Kádár, whereby in Hungary, in sharp contrast with post-1968 Czechoslovakia, there was a form of socialist market economy and a degree of cultural liberalisation, but all under the watchful eye of the ruling party and falling far short of political pluralism. Yet before the end of the 1980s the Cold War was over and, in rapid succession, the East European countries became independent and non-communist without a Soviet soldier firing a shot in anger. Within the Soviet Union itself there was no inkling in 1985, even in the Baltic republics or Ukraine, that this might be the beginning of a process which would see them becoming independent states. Before that happened there was some bloodshed, but on a very small scale in comparison not only with earlier years but also with what has occurred in post-Soviet Russia.

How decisive, then, was Mikhail Gorbachev's role in bringing about such a dramatic transformation of Soviet domestic and foreign policy and of the international political scene? Did systemic crisis force reform on the Soviet leadership or did Gorbachev's reforms create the crisis? How did his political views evolve? To what extent was Gorbachev swept along by forces he could not control? Which outcomes of 1991 did he intend or foresee? What are the implications of answers to these questions for his place in history? These are large issues which I have addressed at much greater length elsewhere (Brown, 1996), but new information relevant to them continues to become available (for example Gorbachev, 1995; 1996; Chernyaev, 1997; Dobrynin, 1996; Ligachev, 1998; Matlock, 1996; Palazchenko, 1997; Vorotnikov, 1995).

Gorbachev is still widely admired in the West but is held in similarly high esteem only by a small, although reflective, minority in the former Soviet Union. In Russia he is the object of criticism (in some cases the hatred) of communists, nationalists, dogmatic marketeers, Boris Yeltsin and post-Soviet placemen. For all the millions of words that have been written about Gorbachev, it is difficult to think of an outstanding leader of transition about whom there are more misconceptions or who has been more misrepresented, not least in his own country.

On the one side there are many people (especially in Russia) who say that he was in thrall to the West, that he betrayed his country and was ready to abandon principles, territory and resources and become a tool of capitalism. On the other side there are those (particularly in the United States) who accuse him of never abandoning Marxist–Leninist beliefs, of being prepared for only half-hearted reforms and of remaining a communist by conviction. In between are scholars who find Gorbachev guilty of inconsistency and who suffer from the illusion that by so doing they have rebutted the arguments of those who see him as a genuinely great reformer.

A leader elected to preserve and strengthen a particular system could not transform that regime, and undermine its powerful defenders, while revealing his hand or speaking frankly at every stage of the process, or by achieving consistency of utterance over time. Thus it makes no contribution to understanding to seize on statements in Gorbachev's speeches critical of political pluralism (when he was saying something else to trusted allies and acting in accordance with those beliefs) or in which Gorbachev downplays his own initial reformism, and to pay no heed to context and the political exigencies of the moment. Not every statement made by Gorbachev during his years in power can be taken entirely at face value. Transforming an ideocratic and highly authoritarian system required constant manoeuvre and different messages for different audiences at different times. While it is not difficult to find radically reformist statements from Gorbachev at all stages of his leadership and especially from 1988 onwards – for it was in that year that he moved from being a reformer of the Soviet system to a systemic transformer (Gorbachev, 1995; Brown, 1996; Shakhnazarov, 1993) – his actions spoke louder than words.

Gorbachev's political evolution

How, when and to what extent Gorbachev's views evolved is a more interesting question than to ask whether he was a communist or a capitalist. Such a crude dichotomy does not, of course, exhaust the range of alternatives. While from his student days and his early years as a Komsomol (Young Communist League) and Communist Party official, Gorbachev displayed more of a mind of his own than was common in those times, he was for many years a relatively orthodox communist. Born into a peasant family in southern Russia, he had, by dint of hard physical work (helping his father bring in a record harvest, for which he received the Order of Red Banner of Labour), intelligence and excellent marks at school – rather than through family connections – been admitted to Moscow University. He entered its law faculty in 1950 and, after completing the normal, five-year course, graduated with distinction in 1955. While he was there he met and married a fellow student, Raisa Titorenko. If that was overwhelmingly the most important event in his personal life (for his relationship with his wife has remained to this day an exceptionally close and devoted one), the most momentous political event (for it very quickly produced a lightening of the atmosphere both in the university and the broader society) was the death of Stalin in March 1953. Upon graduation, Gorbachev was not offered an appointment in Moscow, but he had, nevertheless, a choice between a political or Soviet-style legal career. The system had, it seemed, worked for him, and such social mobility was not so untypical for those times. The beneficiaries of it were, moreover, kept in ignorance of the extent of social, political and economic change in Western Europe, and were therefore all the more inclined to be grateful for the advantages the Soviet system had bestowed on them.

By the early 1980s, in contrast, Gorbachev knew much more about the realities of the Soviet system and of the achievements of the West, although he idealised neither the one nor the other. He had become aware of the need for significant reform of the Soviet system, especially of its economy. When he succeeded Konstantin Chernenko as party leader in March 1985 he believed that to change the Soviet system radically for the better was both possible and desirable. To those who studied carefully the long and critical speech he made at a Moscow conference on ideology in December 1984, he had signalled that the time for complacency was over (Gorbachev, 1984; Brown, 1985). Yet only a few people close to Gorbachev (among them Alexander Yakovlev) realised that he had very serious reformist intentions. That is not to say that Gorbachev's views in 1985 were the same as they had become two or three years later. On the contrary. During his years as the top Soviet leader Gorbachev's learning process continued and his political thinking developed. He moved from being a communist reformer to a socialist of an essentially West European social-democratic type.

Gorbachev's foreign travel, particularly to Western Europe, both before and especially after he became general secretary, contributed to his reassessment, on the one hand, of Soviet history and, on the other, of the legacy of Western social and liberal democracy. His conversations with leading social democrats, not least Willy Brandt and Felipe Gonzalez, were a significant influence on him, as was the evidence of his own eyes when he compared the political authoritarianism and economic inefficiency of the Soviet Union with the greater liberty and prosperity of the West. To see Gorbachev's political and intellectual journey in terms of evolution from true-believing communist student to hard-working and pragmatic regional party official and then, as his horizons and possibilities widened, from communist reformer to social democrat is a key to understanding both the path traversed by Gorbachev and his own gradually changing conception of where he was going.

Far more than Third World authoritarian regimes, the Soviet system had sophisticated defences against any attempt to change it from within or without. The stream of dissidents had been reduced to a trickle by the mid-1980s as a result of the efficiency of the KGB and the hierarchy of rewards and punishments the system offered as an incentive for conformism and disincentive to overt dissent. The Communist Party machine and the KGB had also been very successful in ensuring that no-one of critical views could reach a position where he or she could pose a danger to the regime. Gorbachev, as party first secretary for the Stavropol territory, had impressed a number of senior officials with his energy and intelligence – among them his patron Fedor Kulakov, a former first secretary in Stavropol who had risen to a senior position in the Politburo; the KGB head Yury Andropov, a native of the Stavropol area who enjoyed long conversations with Gorbachev when he regularly holidayed in the spas of the region; the long-serving and highly influential senior party secretary, Mikhail Suslov; and, eventually, an ailing Brezhnev.

Although Andropov realised that Gorbachev was likely to be, within limits, a reformer, he clearly did not worry that this energetic and intelligent party secretary from his home territory might transgress those limits in ways which would place the Soviet system in mortal danger. The only concern of Brezhnev's right-hand man, Chernenko, was a narrower one. He sought to be sure that Gorbachev would be loyal to Brezhnev when Kulakov died in 1978 and the issue of replacing him as Central Committee secretary responsible for agriculture arose. Gorbachev had the support of both Suslov and Andropov for promotion to that post and hence a place in the top leadership team in Moscow. Chernenko called Gorbachev to his office and told him: 'Leonid Ilyich [Brezhnev] proceeds from the assumption that you are on his side and will be loyal to him. He values that' (Gorbachev, 1995, vol. 1, p. 16). Brezhnev never forgot or forgave disloyalty and, albeit gradually and circumspectly, had removed from the leadership all potential rivals. Chernenko, for his part, may have hoped that Gorbachev would be on *his* side when Brezhnev finally departed.

Gorbachev read widely when he was in Stavropol – both Western books in translation and the Soviet literary and political journals. Internally, he was far from as conformist as Chernenko assumed. Moreover he supported Andropov – whom he saw as the most capable contender and a moderate reformer – rather than Chernenko when Brezhnev died. But he had a facility for establishing a rapport with people of diverse personalities and very different views from his own, as he was later to demonstrate when he formed good personal relations with politicians as far removed from Suslov and Andropov as Ronald Reagan and Margaret Thatcher. He had also acquired the self-discipline and self-censorship which were essential attributes for anyone who was tempted by independent thought but who wished to rise up the party hierarchy.

The party apparatus was, in general, no place for people who put a high value on intellectual autonomy, although it included many talented individuals as well as much dead wood. Yet even while Brezhnev was still alive, Gorbachev – especially after he had added in 1980 full membership of the Politburo to his secretaryship of the Central Committee – consulted social scientists with ideas for reform. While he would often agree with quite radical proposals for change made in private seminars, he would somewhat water down these proposals before submitting them to the Secretariat or Politburo, after which they were almost invariably diluted further. Thus, although many of the party intellectuals who encountered Gorbachev in the first half of the 1980s regarded him as an unusual Central Committee secretary because he was quick on the uptake, read books and was interested in ideas, he played by the rules of the game of the party apparatus and did not rock the boat. Only in such a way could a reformer eventually emerge as general secretary. To do so he required the support of two selectorates, the Politburo and the Central Committee, whose members constituted the narrower and broader oligarchies which ruled the Soviet Union. The vast majority of them were concerned, above all, to preserve their own powers and privileges and the system which sustained them.

As he was to display to the full once he became general secretary, Gorbachev in fact had an unusually open mind – even by international political standards, not to speak of the norms of the Communist Party of the Soviet Union. Accordingly, he had to keep this attribute under strict control as he moved up the political ladder. Reflecting on his move from Stavropol to Moscow in 1978, Gorbachev observed: 'I understood that to begin changes in our country was possible only from above' (Gorbachev, 1995, vol. 1, p. 170). Basing his judgement both on his collaboration with Gorbachev in the first half of the 1980s and Gorbachev's subsequent behaviour as general secretary, Nikolay Ryzhkov (chairman of the Soviet Council of Ministers, 1985–90) could aptly observe that Gorbachev had been 'an alien in Brezhnev's Central Committee' (Ryzhkov, 1992, p. 79).

The system should, in fact, have been able to reject Gorbachev at an earlier stage. The gatekeepers of political power in the Kremlin ought to have seen him coming and warned their masters. Some of them – such as Chernenko's aide, Vadim Pechenev (who was alarmed by Gorbachev's rise and rise between 1978 and 1985) – tried to do this, but Gorbachev invariably outsmarted them (Pechenov, 1991). Since Gorbachev had gained the confidence of such senior Politburo members as Suslov (who died in 1982) and Andropov (who died in 1984 after just fifteen months in the general secretaryship), and at least acceptance by Brezhnev (who died in 1982 after eighteen years as party leader), ultra-orthodox, more junior officials in the Central Committee apparatus had to tread carefully in opposing him.

Yet Gorbachev simply could not have risen to the most powerful post within the Soviet system had the extent and intensity of his reformism progressed other than gradually. All attempts, whether from within the party or outside it, to propose radical political reform had resulted at best in blighting the careers of their advocates, or at worst in their exile or imprisonment. The system was such that the best chance of changing it lay in a genuine reformer finding himself in the top rung of the party hierarchy, the office which had more political resources at the disposal of its incumbent than any other. So unlikely did such an outcome seem that most Russian dissidents, prominent among them Alexander Solzhenitsyn, scoffed at the very idea that this was even remotely possible.

It was not the efforts of dissidents, foreign pressure or even the failure of the Soviet system which brought Gorbachev to power, but the fact that he was the *de facto* second secretary to Chernenko when the latter died and there was no other plausible candidate around. The 70–year-old Moscow first secretary, Viktor Grishin, aspired to the job, but after the deaths of three party leaders in as many years, his age, and that of most of his Politburo colleagues, had become a serious disadvantage. Grigory Romanov, a younger man who was, like Gorbachev, a full member of the Politburo and a secretary of the Central Committee, would have been ready to support Grishin in the hope that he could be *his* successor.

There was indeed, on the part of some of the Soviet leaders, apprehension about Gorbachev's coming to power. But this was more because they feared for their personal positions than because they imagined that he would change the political system fundamentally. Shortly before Chernenko's death, the aged chairman of the Council of Ministers, Nikolay Tikhonov, tried to convince the head of the State Security Committee, Viktor Chebrikov, that it would be intolerable if Gorbachev were to become general secretary (Gorbachev, 1995, vol. 1, p. 266). Chebrikov, who had been close to Andropov when the latter headed the KGB, was at that time a Gorbachev supporter (though later he was to be appalled by the radicalism of his reforms) and duly passed on to Gorbachev Tikhonov's remarks. (Gorbachev, who was often accused by his opponents in his last years in office of indecisiveness, showed no indecision in dismissing Grishin, Romanov and Tikhonov from the Politburo within his first year as party leader.)

Nevertheless, since it was obvious to all members of the Politburo that there was no serious alternative candidate to Gorbachev when Chernenko died, every member of that body, including Grishin, Romanov and Tikhonov, spoke in his favour at the decisive Politburo meeting on 11 March 1985. Those present had everything to lose from opposing a certain victor. For some of them, though, little was gained by a late conversion to the winning side.

While Gorbachev made a number of bad appointments during his years at the top, he also made some which changed the balance of influence, and later the balance of power, within the system in favour of reformers. He did this with great finesse, finding the right combination of boldness and caution to strengthen the position of reformers within the leadership during his first four years as Soviet leader. Changing the balance of influence was easiest, inasmuch as Gorbachev had a free hand in appointing his own aides – among whom Anatoly Chernyaev and Georgy Shakhnazarov were to play especially constructive and influential roles – and in choosing which specialists he should listen to. Changing the balance of power, in the sense of altering the composition of the Politburo and the Secretariat of the Central Committee, required the approval of the Politburo itself. A general secretary did not have the absolute right to choose members of the Soviet equivalent of a Cabinet which an American president or British prime minister possesses. Nevertheless, in the hierarchical Soviet system the general secretary was accorded enormous respect and deference, and in practice had a substantial power of patronage. Thus Gorbachev was able to give Alexander Yakovlev, a committed reformer, extraordinarily speedy promotion. Yakovlev was not even a candidate member of the Central Committee in 1985. That meant that, in principle, there were several hundred people ahead of him in the political pecking order. But by the summer of 1987 he was a full member of the Politburo as well as a secretary of the Central Committee and, thanks entirely to Gorbachev's backing, one of the four most powerful people in the country.

The respect which was accorded the holder of the office of general secretary worked to Gorbachev's advantage during the first half of his leadership, when he could, paradoxically, rely on that traditional authority to introduce policies which broke sharply with past Soviet practice. Even when a number of these measures aroused concern within the Soviet establishment, the norms of the system were such that resistance remained covert rather than (at this stage) develop into open criticism. That was especially crucial in the run-up to and during the nineteenth party conference, held in the summer of 1988. This was a turning point both for Gorbachev and Russia. It marked the stage at which he accepted that reform within the parameters of the Soviet system would not work, and that the system itself had to be comprehensively transformed. Of the many important choices made then none were more important than the decision to move to competitive elections for a new legislature, the Congress of People's Deputies. That assembly was duly elected in 1989. A majority, although not all, of the seats were contested by two or more candidates, and the legislature soon showed that it would be no pushover for the executive by refusing to endorse nine out of the sixty-nine ministers or chairmen of state committees proposed to it by the chairman of the Council of Ministers (Ryzhkov, 1992, p. 291). Whatever the limitations of the Congress of People's Deputies and the new-style Supreme Soviet which it elected as an inner body (meeting for eight months of the year, in contrast with the old Supreme Soviet which was in session for less than a week annually), this was a dramatic breakthrough in terms of both political pluralism and executive accountability.

Gorbachev's role in socio-political context

If one examines the other members of the Politburo at the time Gorbachev was chosen as party leader, looking both at their previous and subsequent records, it is clear that none would have pursued the radically new policies both at home and abroad which Gorbachev introduced. In fact, sooner or later all of these Politburo members clashed with Gorbachev and even some who were initially supportive subsequently became severe critics. It is often suggested that the Soviet Union in the 1980s had no alternative to radical change because of its relative economic failure and stagnating authoritarian regime. But economic failure and inflexibly oppressive regimes are very common throughout the world. It is of the essence of an authoritarian regime that, by virtue of the very authoritarian methods it espouses – and its rejection of such devices as free speech, a pluralistic press, opinion polling and contested elections – it can be sustained over many decades. Iraq, Haiti, Zaire (the Congo) and – in the communist world – North Korea are just a few obvious cases in point.

Of course it would be nonsense to attribute systemic transformation to the role of Gorbachev alone. The Soviet Union faced serious problems by the mid-1980s. There had been a long-term decline in the rate of economic growth, with virtual stagnation in the early 1980s. There were many depressing social indicators, such as a lower birth rate, adult males dying younger, a high incidence of alcoholism and drunkenness, and severe environmental degradation. Yet a country can live, however uncomfortably, with such problems. In post-Soviet Russia, in all of the above-mentioned economic and social respects, the statistics (and the reality) have become much worse. Even so the same Russian president, Boris Yeltsin, first elected in 1991, was still in office in 1999, albeit with dramatically diminished authority and support.

There was pull as well as push for reform. Generational change was one important factor. That does not mean that young people were in the forefront of the movement for change in the second half of the 1980s. In *post*-Soviet Russia they are the generational group most optimistic about the future and least inclined to support a return to anything resembling the communist system, but there was no student revolution or radical youth movement during the years between 1985 and 1990 which saw the political transformation of the Soviet Union. Indeed, among the key reformers, people in their fifties and early sixties were disproportionately well represented. This can partly be explained by the fact that for the first four years after Gorbachev succeeded Chernenko this was a revolution from above. Younger people were rarely found in the senior positions within Communist Party or Academy of Sciences research institutes which afforded them access to policy makers. It was also, however, a matter of *political generations*. Two terms used to describe the people who were at the heart of the reform movement were 'children of the Twentieth Congress' and *shestidesyatniki*.

The first of these descriptions refers to the party congress in 1956, at which Nikita Khrushchev was bold enough to draw attention to some of the crimes of Stalin, thus raising questions in the minds of the more thoughtful Soviet citizens about the defects of a system which had allowed Stalin to get away with his monstrous abuse of power. On the whole these were younger, educated people in their twenties or early thirties, who were readier than the older generation to reassess their previous convictions and had spent less of their politically conscious lives being socialised along Stalinist lines. The term, *shestidesyatniki* was first coined in the nineteenth century to describe the reformers of the 1860s. It came to be used for the political generation a century later who, stimulated by Khrushchev's anti-Stalinism, looked for further changes in the Soviet Union of the 1960s. They were to be disappointed, for the ruling oligarchy asserted itself against the erratic Khrushchev in 1964 and replaced him with an ultra-cautious top leadership firmly opposed (particularly in the person of Brezhnev) to taking the risks involved in serious reform. It was this generation which was given a second chance, and far greater opportunity to influence policy, when one of its representatives, Gorbachev – who was in his mid-twenties when Khrushchev delivered his February 1956 'secret speech' and had just turned fifty-four when he became general secretary – came to power.

More generally, the social forces which could be mobilised in support of political liberalisation and subsequent democratisation, as well as concessions to the market, were very different in the mid-1980s from what they had been a generation earlier when Khrushchev succeeded Stalin as party leader. Educational standards had risen and there was a large professional class of people with higher education. Their knowledge of the outside world, while less extensive than it was to become as a result of Gorbachev's policy of *glasnost* was far superior to that possessed by the same social stratum at the time of Stalin's death. This intelligentsia, defined in sociological rather than moral terms, provided a social base to which Gorbachev and his allies could appeal. Two of his closest colleagues, who acquired widespread popularity with the intelligentsia both for the policies they espoused and their relative openness, were Alexander Yakovlev and Eduard Shevardnadze. They were among Gorbachev's most successful appointments. Even senior officials in the Central Committee, as well as the entire staff of the Ministry of Foreign Affairs were astonished when in the summer of 1985 Gorbachev named the first secretary of the Georgian Communist Party, Shevardnadze, as foreign minister (Chernyaev, 1993, p. 49). Notwithstanding a total lack of previous foreign policy experience, Shevardnadze performed his new duties with flair and distinction. The most decisive initiator of the new foreign policy was Gorbachev himself, with Yakovlev, Chernyaev and Yevgeny Primakov among his key advisers. His appointments in this field were made with the need for new approaches in international relations firmly in mind. As an executant of a radically different foreign policy, marked by such unusual attributes in the Soviet context as goodwill and sincerity, Shevardnadze was able to establish qualitatively different relations with his Western counterparts from those achieved by his predecessor, the dour and highly conservative Gromyko.

There were, then, factors conducive to change in the Soviet Union of 1985. Yet there was no civil society in which independent organisations could defend their interests and viewpoints and mount

pressure for reform. The initiative for reform came from an enlightened minority of party officials and party intellectuals whose hand
was enormously strengthened by the arrival of a like-minded person
in the Kremlin. Gorbachev's own initial assumption was that intra-
system reforms would be enough to produce intensified economic
growth and what he called 'democratisation'. At that time what he
meant by the latter term was a degree of liberalisation and more mean-
ingful popular participation rather than pluralist democracy
(Gorbachev, 1984). There *was* no crisis in the Soviet Union in 1985.
When Chernenko died the political succession proceeded smoothly,
and there was widespread approval in the country that a capable,
younger man had finally taken over from the gerontocrats. Wherever
he went in 1985, Gorbachev was greeted by large and spontaneously
enthusiastic crowds. Even his political opponents, with the
predictable exception of Boris Yeltsin, acknowledge that in his earlier
years as general secretary, Gorbachev was a popular leader. Indeed,
contrary to conventional wisdom, the most reliable opinion polls of
the time show that it was as late as May 1990, more than five years
into his leadership, that Gorbachev was overtaken by Yeltsin as the
most popular politician both in Russia and the USSR as a whole
(Brown, 1996, pp. 10–11, 270–1, 381). The Soviet Union was faced
with slow and relative decline, but that is a very different matter from
systemic crisis.

If some youthful regeneration of the regime had been introduced in
the mid-1980s as a substitute for radical reform, this would not have
solved the long-term problems of the Soviet state, but there is no good
reason to suppose that the system would not have survived into the
next century. People grumbled, but there were no mass protests or any
serious opposition until Gorbachev made the Soviet Union safe for
dissent. By attempting first to liberalise and then (from 1988) to
democratise, Gorbachev did in fact create crisis – whereby the very
survival both of the system and the multinational Soviet state was
thrown into doubt. All the suppressed grievances of decades, especially nationalist grievances, came to the surface, and since Gorbachev
eschewed the kind of harsh and sustained use of force which might
have stopped the protests in their tracks, the oppositional forces ultimately prevailed. His own preference for having viable new
institutions in place before transferring all the powers of the party
apparatus to them – and for movement from pseudo-federalism to a
genuine federation as a way of renewing and preserving the Soviet
state – was overtaken by events. Indeed, in his last two and a half years

in office he was swept along, and eventually aside, by forces he could not control. But until the first elections for the new legislature – the Congress of People's Deputies of the USSR – in the early summer of 1989, Gorbachev was in the vanguard of reform and, to an extent which in retrospect may seem surprising, still in control of the direction of change, and to a certain extent its pace.

One of the questions raised earlier was that of which outcomes in the transformation of the Soviet Union Gorbachev intended or foresaw. Since his views were evolving in a complex process of political learning, there is no simple answer to this. His aspirations were different in 1988 from what they had been in 1985.What is absolutely clear, however, is that at no time did he intend the break-up of the Soviet Union. He wanted a genuine federation, not disintegration. He underestimated the strength of national discontent in the Baltic republics in particular, and the fact that almost every nationality had its own profound reasons for discontent which the new tolerance and freedoms of the Gorbachev era allowed them to air publicly. It is probable that a smaller and looser federation could have been held together – minus the Baltic states – if various political actors had behaved differently. But this did not depend on Gorbachev alone. The putschists of August 1991, in their attempt to oust Gorbachev, preserve the union and return the system to the *status quo ante*, in fact accelerated the break-up of the Soviet Union. So did Yeltsin by playing the Russian card against 'the centre' and putting his own struggle to get Gorbachev out of the Kremlin, and himself inside as the sole master of all he surveyed, well ahead of preserving as much of the old union as possible.

However Gorbachev, who had been the first Soviet politician to use the term 'pluralism' other than pejoratively when he spoke in 1987 of the need for a 'socialist pluralism' and a 'pluralism of opinion' (Brown, 1996, p. 127), did favour a pluralisation of the political system. The first time he publicly endorsed 'political pluralism' as distinct from 'socialist pluralism' was in February 1990, but in private he had accepted by the summer of 1988 that this was the direction in which the Soviet Union must move. Endorsing the idea of contested elections for a new legislature, he realised that they would lead in due course to the emergence of competing political parties and a more fully fledged political pluralism. By that time there was already substantial freedom of speech, growing freedom of the press, extensive interest group activity and religious tolerance.

Above all, the ending of the Cold War was one of Gorbachev's main aims from the outset of his general secretaryship. As one instance of his commitment to this, he made clear to the Politburo as early as 17 October 1985 that Soviet troops must leave Afghanistan, and the sooner the better (Chernyaev, 1993, p. 57; Dobrynin, 1996, p. 442). It was, however, in 1988 that he expounded (in his speech at the nineteenth party conference in June and UN speech in December) on the right of citizens of every state to choose what political and economic system they would live under. By willing the means he in effect willed the end of communist regimes in Eastern Europe, even if the speed with which that occurred took him by surprise. He remained true to his principle of allowing those former Soviet client states to become independent and non-communist if their peoples so chose.

Obstacles and incentives

Some of the obstacles to change have already been touched upon. One of the most serious was that any liberalisation, not to speak of democratisation, in the multinational Soviet state was bound to place the preservation of the union under enormous strain. Historical memories and contemporary grievances aside, this had an institutional dimension. The Soviet Union was administratively organised along national-territorial lines. Each of the fifteen union republics bore the name of the particular nationality living in its historic homeland. So long as the institutions which were nominally under the jurisdiction of those republics were in fact closely controlled by a highly centralised and disciplined Communist Party and subject to the surveillance of powerful security organs, the concessions to national sentiment embodied in the administrative structure posed no serious threat to the union or the general secretary. From the moment, however, that contested elections were introduced, local politicians had to pay as much or more attention to the views of their republican electorates as to those of the Communist Party leadership in Moscow. Thus in a republic such as Lithuania, where there were strong pressures for independence, even the first secretary of the Communist Party, Algirdas-Mikolas Brazauskas, found himself espousing the national cause and clashing with Moscow.

For Gorbachev, the creation of legislatures with real powers both in the republics and at the all-union level, coexisting with an undermined central economic apparatus, a weakened party apparatus and increasing anxiety and anger on the part of the security forces and army, meant his subjection to almost intolerable cross-pressures.

There was no way he could satisfy one constituency without offending another. His major political reforms, enunciated in 1988 and introduced over the next two years, meant that by late 1990 he was displeasing virtually all of the institutional actors. In the winter of 1990–91 he made a tactical retreat and tried to occupy a centrist position at a time of increased polarisation of political forces, but to no avail, and by the spring of 1991 he was adopting an ever more openly social-democratic position.

In his earliest years as party leader Gorbachev would have preferred change to have come quicker. In his last years in office he would happily have settled for a slower tempo of change. Taking his years in power as a whole, he was a systemic transformer who favoured a somewhat more gradual transformation of the political and economic system. It is hard, however, to see how, after the crucial democratising and pluralising steps had been taken, *anyone* could have regulated the speed of developments. By definition, once he had rewritten the rules of the Soviet game the general secretary could not control the pace of change in the way that had been possible for Brezhnev, Andropov or even Chernenko (by authorising no change at all), or as Gorbachev himself, by orchestrating innovation, had done during his first years as general secretary. It is very much to Gorbachev's credit that he consciously gave up a number of his levers of power as general secretary and increasingly relied on the power of persuasion. When that proved insufficient, it was at least as important that he did not attempt to turn the clock back by declaring a state of emergency and using the security forces to restore 'order'. He was constantly being urged by the KGB and many within the Communist Party to take this action, but although Gorbachev listened to their arguments he consistently refrained from adopting such measures, which would have been the beginning of the end of the reform process.

One reason for Gorbachev's resistance to declaring a state of emergency was his genuine revulsion against rule by violence and coercion. He was the first Soviet leader to realise that means were as important as ends in politics. Indeed one of his prime achievements was to introduce politics as an activity to the citizens of the Soviet Union. Previously there had been court intrigues, bureaucratic rivalries, patron–client relations and at times mass mobilisation, but many of the more essential features of democratic politics were totally absent. Apart from Gorbachev's deep-seated personal values, the arguments of interlocutors both in Moscow and abroad significantly influenced his political ideas and led him gradually to embrace a social-democratic interpretation of socialism. Gorbachev was a leader for whom ideas mattered, and any attempt to explain his policies entirely on the basis of self-interest is doomed to failure. Indeed if he had wanted nothing more than power, privilege and constant praise in the mass media, he had no need to embark on a process of reform in the first place. Even such a nonentity of a political leader as Konstantin Chernenko was able to rely on the deference of his colleagues and subordinates, and on a chorus of praise from the Soviet press, until his dying day.

Once, moreover, Gorbachev had gone down the road of liberalisation and democratisation he had other incentives not to retreat. Convinced that the path he had chosen was the right one, he had, for one thing, his place in history to consider. Moreover, Gorbachev was intelligent enough to know that if he turned his back on political pluralism, as he was under pressure to do from a majority within the party and state apparatus – including, not least, the regional and local party secretaries – he would not be forgiven for endangering the system to the extent he had. A Gorbachev who put himself at the disposal of the party apparatus would be a Gorbachev who would rapidly be disposed of. Finally, from the outset of his leadership he had been acutely conscious of the linkage between domestic and foreign policy. He was aware that to oppress dissidents and to use the massive force which would be required to dampen down national passions, once they had been aroused, would undermine all of his achievements in the realm of East–West relations. The respect and goodwill of Western leaders, which he valued, would be lost. The Cold War, which in the view of US Secretary of State George Shultz was over by 1988 (Shultz, 1993, p. 1138), would have been relaunched.

If in the last two years of his leadership Gorbachev faced the constant danger of his reforms getting out of hand, his first two or three years had been dominated by the struggle to get them off the ground. Both the economic ministries – which at least until very late in the Soviet era when they began to see opportunities, under a possible new economic order, for owning the property they had formerly administered (Whitefield, 1993, p. 266) – and the Communist Party apparatus feared that economic and political reform would remove many of their functions and undermine their powers. Gorbachev's first struggles with the bureaucracy were directed at the ministerial system, but his more important endeavour, launched in 1988, was to transfer power from the party apparatus to elected state bodies. This aroused fierce opposition. Entirely representative of the view of his conservative communist critics, and a reflection of their bitterness, is the statement in the memoirs of former KGB Chairman, Vladimir Kryuchkov: 'His [Gorbachev's] secret striving to destroy the Communist Party of the Soviet Union was crowned with success because at the head of the party stood a traitor and, along with him, a row of his associates who were engaged in that treacherous cause' (Kryuchkov, 1996, vol. 2, p. 360). Another former close colleague in the Politburo (who had known Gorbachev ever since they had over-lapped as students at Moscow University), Anatoly Lukyanov, declared flatly: 'Gorbachev betrayed his party' (*Ogonek*, 1995). To this common accusation another former Politburo member, Vadim Medvedev, who remained loyal to Gorbachev, responded that by the spring of 1991 it was clear that the Communist Party would have to split into 'reformist and conservative-fundamentalist' camps. Discussions, he pointed out (as has Gorbachev himself), were already underway about making such a break later in the year, but the August putsch put an end to all that. 'When', Medvedev continued, 'my former colleagues speak about Gorbachev's betrayal, I ask them: why was it that in August 1991 neither the Politburo nor the Secretariat of the Central Committee, nor the local party organizations, found the courage to demand the release of Gorbachev' from house arrest on the Crimean coast (*Ogonek*, 1995).

Gorbachev's legacy and achievements

By pursuing pluralising reforms Gorbachev was purposefully destroy-ing both the unity and the monopoly of power of the Communist Party. On that at least, both those in Russia who still esteem him highly and his hard-line communist enemies can agree, however differently they evaluate the outcome. Political freedom and political pluralism are two of Gorbachev's greatest legacies, as was his break with the communist style of politics – dogmatic, uncompromising and confrontational. Writing on the eightieth anniversary of the October Revolution of 1917, Gorbachev emphasised that first the Bolsheviks and later Stalin had demonstrated the impossibility of building democracy on the basis of hatred or as a result of the liqui-dation of one part of society by another (Gorbachev, 1997, pp. 91–2).

No less momentous an achievement was the removal of the threat of nuclear war – which could have come about by accident as well as design – between the two military superpowers. Gorbachev was the key player in ending the Cold War. He was the fourth general secretary to overlap with the presidency of Ronald Reagan, and nothing changed for the better until he became Soviet leader. During Reagan's first term of office (1980–84) international tension was acute and East European independence remote. Soviet policy was primarily to blame for this state of affairs, but according to Anatoly Dobrynin (Soviet ambassador to the United States from 1962 to 1986 and subsequently head of the International Department of the Central Committee), 'the impact of Reagan's hard-line policy on the internal debates in the Kremlin and on the evolution of the Soviet leadership was exactly the opposite from the one intended by Washington' (Dobrynin, 1996, p. 482). It was the changes introduced by Gorbachev in both domestic and foreign policy – 'new thinking' followed by new behaviour – which persuaded not only Margaret Thatcher but also Ronald Reagan that this was a man they could 'do business with'.

Against that, the unintended consequences of Gorbachev's reforms have to be considered. The loss of military superpower status may not be hard to bear for the average citizen in the former Soviet Union, but the armed services and military industry were huge employers in its Slavic heartlands. Those who worked in that sphere enjoyed many privileges. Not all of them, to put it mildly, regard enhanced freedom as an adequate substitute for lost prestige and vanished economic and social security. Where people stand on Gorbachev depends on where they sit. For a Russian pensioner, whose allowance in post-Soviet Russia has been paid late or sometimes not at all, the Brezhnev years have acquired a glow which was less visible at the time. Gorbachev is frequently blamed for the pain of economic transition inflicted even in the years since he left office.

While much of what Gorbachev is now castigated for is the responsibility of his successors, the economy can indeed be seen as a relative failure of Gorbachev's leadership, in comparison at least with the successful liberalisation and democratisation of the political system and his achievements in foreign policy. At the time when he left office the Soviet economic system was in limbo. Concessions had been made to the market, but neither the instruments of the old command economy nor the new market mechanisms were fully in place, and the shops were emptier in 1991 than they had been in 1985. As post-Soviet Russian governments have discovered, however, there is no way the wrongly developed, rather than underdeveloped, Russian economy can be transformed smoothly. The pain of the majority (combined with an improvement for a minority, and previously undreamt-of riches for a few) has increased in the years since

Gorbachev was in power. While the first tentative steps towards the market and a mixed economy were taken under Gorbachev, the liberalisation of prices and large-scale privatisation (with state assets sold for a song) got seriously under way only from 1992 when Boris Yeltsin gave young economic reformers their heads.

In this respect, and in this respect alone, Yeltsin could lay reasonable claim to be the leader of the Russian transition, although he has often claimed much more. In reality the key decisions which brought about the transformation of the Soviet political system were taken in 1988 when Yeltsin had lost his seat as a candidate member of the Politburo and played no part in the decision-making. Equally, he had nothing whatsoever to do with the formulation or implementation of the new thinking on foreign policy which transformed East–West relations. That Gorbachev is an incomparably more significant historical figure than Yeltsin (which is not of course to say that Yeltsin has been inconsequential) was lost on some observers during Gorbachev's travails of 1990–91, which coincided with Yeltsin's growing domestic popularity. But the real leader of the Russian transition from a highly authoritarian communist system to political pluralism and from Cold War confrontation to international cooperation was Gorbachev.

Gorbachev left Russia a freer country than it had ever been, and that will be his lasting legacy. While the danger of relapse into authoritarian rule cannot be totally discounted, it is unlikely that Russians will ever allow themselves to be as unfree as they were before Gorbachev arrived on the scene. The difference that Gorbachev made is seen starkly by some. The author of an article in the Writers' Union weekly newspaper in late 1995 declared: 'Gorbachev freed the people from slavery, and in this he can be compared with the Tsar-Liberator Alexander II putting an end to serfdom' (*Literaturnaya gazeta*, 1995). One of the more remarkable evaluations of Gorbachev was given in the same year by Alexander Yakovlev, for though Yakovlev worked closely with Gorbachev during the *perestroika* years they became bitterly estranged in the period that followed, partly because Yakovlev reacted much more positively to the Yeltsin administration and accepted a position within it as head of a state television channel. On the tenth anniversary of Gorbachev's becoming general secretary of the Soviet Communist Party, Yakovlev said: 'I consider Gorbachev to be the greatest reformer of the century, the more so because he tried to do this in Russia where from time immemorial the fate of reformers has been unenviable' (*Ogonek*, 1995).

How Gorbachev will be evaluated by Russians in the immediate years ahead will depend largely on developments beyond his control. His short-term reputation is linked to what happens next in Russia – on whether the post-Soviet rulers have the will and wisdom to combine democratic institution-building and strengthening the rule of law with an economic policy which brings improvement to the lives of a majority of the people. Since the process of change began with Gorbachev, he is more likely to get credit for it from those living in Russia today if their conditions of life get better rather than worse. In a longer historical perspective, though, it will be easier for Russians, seeing how firmly entrenched the oppressive Soviet regime had been and how little hope there appeared of changing it until Gorbachev entered the Kremlin, to recognise the scale of his achievement.

It is often remarked that the communist system was unreformable and, by implication, Gorbachev was foolish to attempt to reform it. But a reformer can introduce change which brings a system to the point where it becomes different in kind. Gorbachev has made clear on many occasions that until 1988 he believed that the Soviet system could be improved by radical reform. From that time onwards he was conscious that it was so fundamentally flawed that it had to be dismantled and replaced by a system of a different type. His reformism, in other words, assumed an increasingly transformative character. All efforts by dissidents to change the Soviet system had ended dismally, however honourable their failure. Any revolutionary attempt to overthrow the regime would have been equally doomed, and the cost in blood would have been high. It was the good fortune of Russia and the rest of the world that Gorbachev was an evolutionary, not a revolutionary, that he bided his time and learned in the process, and that in less than seven years the political map of Europe was changed peacefully to an extent which had previously occurred only after major wars.

Mikhail Gorbachev: chronology

1931, 2 March	Born into a peasant family in the village of Privolnoe in the Stavropol region of southern Russia.
1950–55	Student in the law faculty of Moscow University.
1953	Married Raisa Titorenko, a fellow student at Moscow University.
1955–78	Regional Komsomol and Communist Party official in Stavropol.

1970–78	First secretary of Stavropol regional party organisation.
1971	Member of Central Committee of Communist Party of the Soviet Union.
1978	Moved to Moscow as secretary of the Central Committee.
1979	Candidate member of the Politburo.
1980	Full member of the Politburo,
1984–85	Following death of Yuri Andropov became *de facto* second secretary of the Communist Party under Konstantin Chernenko.
1985, 11 March	Elected general secretary of the CPSU by the Central Committee of the party following the death of Chernenko.
1985, April	Signaled intention to reform the Soviet system (*perestroika*) at Central Committee plenum.
1985, November	Met President Ronald Reagan in Geneva in first Soviet–US summit of the decade.
1986	First clear signs of *glasnost* – a developing openness to criticism and fresh ideas.
1986, October	Summit meeting with Reagan in Reykjavik.
1986, December	Telephoned Academician Andrey Sakharov (in exile since 1980 in the city of Gorky) to tell him he was free to return to Moscow.
1987, January	Political reform announced at plenary session of Central Committee.
1987, June	Economic reform launched at Central Committee plenum.
1987, December	INF Treaty signed at Gorbachev–Reagan summit meeting in Washington.
1988, April	Agreement signed on withdrawal of Soviet troops from Afghanistan.
1988, May	Gorbachev-Reagan summit meeting in Moscow
1988, June–July	Nineteenth Conference of Soviet Communist Party: major political reforms proposed by Gorbachev, including contested elections for new legislature.
1988, December	In a speech to the United Nations, Gorbachev reiterated each country's right to choose its own political and economic system and pledged Soviet non-intervention.
1989, March	Elections for new legislative body, the Congress of People's Deputies of the USSR.
1989, May-June	First session of Congress of People's Deputies.
1989	East European countries gain their independence.
1989, December	Malta summit meeting between Gorbachev and President George Bush.
1990, March	Gorbachev elected president of the USSR by

	Congress of People's Deputies.
1990, March	'Leading role' of Communist Party removed from Soviet Constitution.
1990, summer	Twenty-Eighth Congress of Communist Party of Soviet Union: Boris Yeltsin resigned from Communist Party.
1990, October–1991, March	Gorbachev made tactical retreat under pressure from conservative Communist forces.
1991, June	Yeltsin elected president of Russia.
1991, 18–22 August	Coup attempt by hard-liners to oust Gorbachev as president of USSR
1991, 24 August	Gorbachev resigned as general secretary of Soviet Communist Party.
1991, 8 December	Yeltsin, as Russian president, joined forces with Ukrainian President Kravchuk and Belorussian President Shushkevich to announce replacement of USSR by a 'Commonwealth of Independent States'.
1991, 25 December	Gorbachev resigned as president of the USSR, and the Soviet Union itself ceased to exist.
1992, January	Gorbachev became president of the Gorbachev Foundation, a Moscow think-tank

Notes

1 Grachev (former deputy head of the International Department of the Central Committee of the Soviet Communist Party; in 1991 Presidential Press Spokesman for Gorbachev), in conversation with the author.
2 The late Rita Klímová (née Budinová), also in conversation with the author.

References*

Brown, Archie, (1985), 'Gorbachev: New Man in the Kremlin', *Problems of Communism*, vol. 34, no. 3 (May–June), pp. 1–23.

Brown, Archie (1996), *The Gorbachev Factor* (Oxford and New York: Oxford University Press).

Chernyaev, Anatoliy (1993), *Shest' let s Gorbachevym* ('Six Years with Gorbachev'), (Moscow: Kul'tura).

Chernyaev, Anatoliy (1997), *1991: Dnevnik pomoshchnika Prezidenta SSSR* (1991: The Diary of an aide to the President of the USSR), (Moscow: Respublika).

Dobrynin, Anatoly (1996), *In Confidence: Moscow's ambassador to America's six Cold War presidents (1962–1986)*, (New York: Random House).

Gorbachev, M.S. (1984), *Zhivoe tvorchestvo naroda* (The Living Creativity of the People), Moscow: Politizdat.

Gorbachev, Mikhail (1995) *Zhizn' i reformy* (Life and Reforms), 2 vols (Moscow: Novosti).

* The transliteration of Russian names and titles in the references follows the British standard system. Russian names in the text are loosely based on that system, but modified for the sake of simplicity and familiarity.

Gorbachev, Mikhail (1996) *Memoirs*, (New York and London: Doubleday).

Gorbachev, M. S. (1997), *Razmyshleniya ob Oktyabr'skoy Revolyutsii* (Reflections on the October Revolution), (Moscow: Aprel'-85).

Kryuchkov, Vladimir (1996) *Lichnoe delo* (A Personal Matter), 2 vols (Moscow: Olimp).

Ligachev, E. K. (1998), *Predosterezhenie* (Warning) (Moscow: *Pravda Interneshnl*).

Matlock, Jack F., Jr., (1996), *Autopsy on an Empire: The American Ambassador's account of the collapse of the Soviet Union* (New York: Random House).

Myl'nikov, Aleksandr (1995) 'Gorbachev – vot kto nash Aleksandr II' (Gorbachev – This is our Alexander II), *Literaturnaya gazeta*, 1 November, p. 11.

Ogonek (1995) 'Zagadka Gorbacheva' (The Enigma of Gorbachev), no. 11 (March).

Palazchenko, Pavel (1997) *My Years with Gorbachev and Shevardnadze*, (Philadelpia: Pennsylvania State University Press).

Pechenev, Vadim (1991) *Gorbachev: K vershinam vlasti* (Gorbachev: To the Summit of Power), (Moscow: Gospodin Narod).

Roxburgh, Angus (1991) *The Second Russian Revolution*, (London: BBC Books).

Ryzhkov, Nikolay (1992) *Perestroyka: Istoriya predatel'stv* (Perestroika: A History of Betrayals), (Moscow: Novosti).

Shakhnazarov, Georgiy (1993) *Tsena svobody* (The Price of Freedom) (Moscow: Rossika zevs).

Shultz, George (1993) *Turmoil and Triumph: My Years as Secretary of State* (New York: Macmillan).

Vorotnikov, V. I. (1995) *A bylo eto tak ... Iz dnevnika chlena Politburo* (And That's How It Was ... From the Diary of a Member of the Politburo of the Central Committee of the CPSU] (Moscow: Sovet veteranov knigoizdaniya).

Whitefield, Stephen (1993) *Industrial Power and the Soviet State* (Oxford: Clarendon Press).

F. W. de Klerk

If one has to cut off the tail of a dog, it is much better to do so
with one clean and decisive stroke
(F. W. De Klerk, 1997a, p. 5)

F. W. de Klerk and Nelson Mandela shake hands, shortly before the first all-South Africa democratic elections that will catapult Mandela into national power and lead de Klerk to resign from politics. (*Copyright © EPA–AFP*)

2
F. W. de Klerk: Enlightened Conservative[1]

David Welsh and Jack Spence

If one has to cut off the tail of a dog, it is much better to do so with one clean and decisive stroke (F. W. de Klerk, 1997a, p. 5)

On 2 February 1990, in at atmosphere of fevered expectancy, F. W. de Klerk went to the Cape Town House of Assembly to deliver a long-awaited speech. De Klerk had been careful to hold his full hand close to his chest. Only the cabinet and a few trusted officials knew exactly what the speech would contain. Even his own National Party (NP) caucus would be caught unawares by the sheer scale of the changes that were to follow. Outwardly calm, he turned to his wife, Marike, and said 'South Africa will never be the same again after this.' Within minutes de Klerk had announced the imminent release of Nelson Mandela after 27 years in prison, the lifting of the ban on the African National Congress (ANC) and other proscribed organisations, and a commitment to negotiate a fully democratic constitution. The speech heralded the end of nearly 350 years of white rule in South Africa. De Klerk had decided

> to take a quantum leap.... I knew what I announced would cause great concern to many followers, but decided to announce everything at once, rather than to do so in a piece-meal fashion. That gave us the tremendous advantage of gaining the initiative as opposed to appearing to be giving in to pressure (de Klerk, 1997a, p. 5).

Nothing in de Klerk's past prepared his fellow countrymen (nor indeed South Africa's international critics) for such a 'conversion'. He was not widely known in government circles abroad and his cabinet posts had largely been preoccupied with domestic affairs. He was generally regarded as a conservative. Indeed he owed his position as president largely to that perception, and most commentators thought he would be most likely to tinker with the apartheid system rather than abolish it altogether. What, then, led him to such a dramatic departure?

De Klerk's early political career

Frederik Willem – F. W. – de Klerk was born in Johannesburg in 1936 to a highly political Afrikaner nationalist family. His father was a cabinet minister from 1954 until 1969, and also president of the Senate from 1961 to 1969. The de Klerk family were members of the *Gereformeerde Kerk* (literally, the Reformed Church), colloquially known as the *Dopper* Church. Although the church was theologically fundamentalist and conservative, it is perhaps important to note that, already in the late 1960s, *Dopper* theologians were becoming increasingly critical of apartheid practices which, they maintained, violated Calvinist principles (Hexam, 1981, pp. 192–3).

The young de Klerk attended Potchefstroom University for Christian Higher Education, a *Dopper*-led institution that had historically been closely aligned with Afrikaner nationalism. He read law and graduated with distinction in 1958. The precise impact of specifically *Gereformeerde* doctrines on de Klerk's thinking is hard to gauge, but he clearly relished the logic and precision of the law. His interest in politics flourished in the congenial (for nationalists) environment of Potchefstroom, a small town in what was then the Western Transvaal. He was prominent in student affairs and became actively involved with the NP. In short, de Klerk grew up in a relatively closed environment, intensely nationalist, relatively free from leavening influences,[2] and followed the classic route of young nationalist politicians. He was firmly committed to apartheid, not, he would later insist, because it promised the indefinite perpetuation of a racial order, but because it seemed to offer the only possible way out of the conflict caused by Afrikaner demands for freedom and the rising black challenge to apartheid.[3]

After more than ten years of successful legal practice in the Transvaal town of Vereeniging, de Klerk was offered a professorship in the law faculty at Potchefstroom, but turned this down in favour of becoming a member of parliament. He won a by-election in November 1972 with comparative ease and assumed his seat in parliament. De

Klerk soon made his mark as an outstanding debater and committee man, conscientious about his parliamentary and constituency duties. In the 1970s the Transvaal NP was still the dominant force in the NP, and provincial rivalries remained an important factor. His amiability even towards opponents, his accessibility and helpfulness to colleagues made him popular. He advised another young Transvaal MP, Leon Wessels, who entered parliament in 1978 (and subsequently became a member of de Klerk's cabinet): 'Stay in the background, and don't become involved in faction-forming or internal struggles. Concentrate rather on your constituency and look after it' (Wessels, 1994, p. 5). Clearly, this is what de Klerk himself had done, so much so in fact that where his actual loyalties lay in the internal fights that were to wrack the NP in the late 1970s and after was often a matter for conjecture.

As a rising star in the Transvaal NP of the late 1970s it must have been apparent to de Klerk that stormy waters lay ahead. Not only had there been serious violence in the country during 1976–7, but the NP was shaken to its core by the Information Scandal of 1977–78 (involving allegations of large-scale misuse of funds), which destroyed Vorster's premiership, cost the Minister of Information, Connie Mulder, his post, and, unexpectedly, catapulted P. W. Botha into the prime ministership. Andries Treurnicht meanwhile replaced Mulder as Transvaal NP leader and consolidated his position as leader of the rightwing *verkrampte* (reactionary) nationalists.

Vorster himself had recognised de Klerk's talents and appointed him to the cabinet in April 1978 as minister of posts and telecommunications and of social welfare and pensions. These were not the most important portfolios, but de Klerk was one of the youngest appointees to a NP cabinet ever. Thereafter de Klerk would consecutively hold a succession of ministerial portfolios: sport and recreation; mining and environmental planning; mineral and energy affairs; internal affairs; and national education, which he held up to the time of his election as state president in 1989. In addition to his ministerial responsibilities de Klerk was also to become chairman of the Ministers' Council in the (white) House of Assembly in the tricameral parliament on 1 July 1985.

In 1982 Treurnicht broke away from the National Party with a group of supporters to form the Conservative Party (CP), which at its height enjoyed the support of some 30 per cent of Afrikaner whites. De Klerk was thereupon elected Transvaal leader of the NP. Since he retained a strong commitment to Afrikaner unity, de Klerk regretted the split and indeed tried to prevent it, but once it had happened, damage limitation became his priority as he faced the immediate problem of staunching a potentially serious haemorrhage of support. Treurnicht was a crafty politician whom de Klerk disliked. A fight for possession of Afrikanerdom's soul ensued. The conflict presaged the situation that de Klerk would face in 1990 and after: of having to fight on two fronts, left and right, with redoubtable opponents in both cases.

Although he never hesitated to take on Treurnicht directly, the kind of political straddling act required of de Klerk nurtured CP hopes that he was a closet conservative; *verligtes* (reformists) regarded him with suspicion. In his later comments on this apparent ambiguity de Klerk maintained that it was a strategy designed to protect his right flank. He told Colin Eglin, a leading politician in the liberal Progressive Federal Party and one of the critics of his alleged conservatism, that; 'If you were leader of the National Party, with Andries Treurnicht breathing down your neck, you [Eglin] might even sound like me' (Waldmeir, 1997, p. 25).[4] For himself, F. W. de Klerk denied ever having switched from being *verkrampt* to *verlig*: 'I've remained the same man throughout the whole process' (Kotzé and Geldenhuys, 1990, p. 15). His younger brother described F. W.'s strategy as follows:

> He had deliberately built up a conservative image and a flexible profile. In Afrikaner politics, power is based on conservative thinking; in the long run it gains you confidence, and once you have that, you can do magical things with the Afrikaner. That was FW's strategy, not rigid conservatism. He was pragmatic and ambitious enough to build his image on the middle course between enlightened [*verlig*] and ultra-conservative [*verkrampt*], and he was astute enough to convert his basic reluctance to give offence into a personal style, a strategy that gained him acceptability and influence. Not that he dissimulated; he just followed his political intuition (Willem de Klerk, 1991, p. 22).

Botha's administration

P. W. Botha (prime minister from 1978 to 1983, state president from 1983 to 1989) had made a promising start as a reformer, recognising African trade unions, abandoning the fiction that urban Africans were 'temporary sojourners', allowing property rights to urban Africans, abolishing the hated 'pass laws' (or influx control), which imposed severe restrictions on Africans' freedom of movement, repealing laws that prohibited marriage or sex across the colour line, and accepting, in 1986, that 'the people of the Republic of South Africa make up one nation', although it was 'a nation of minorities' (Welsh, 1994a, pp. 185–6).

The centrepiece of Botha's administration was the tricameral constitution of 1983. This curious piece of constitutional engineering excluded Africans from its purview – they, it was contended, would have to satisfy their political aspirations through the 'homelands'. The Coloured and Indian minority categories were each accorded separate chambers in a three-chamber parliament that would, in effect, be controlled by the white chamber, in which the NP enjoyed a large majority. The operating principle was that 'own affairs' (that is, group-specific matters) would be controlled by the relevant chamber, while 'general affairs' (matters affecting all three groups) had to be passed by all three chambers. The tricameral constitution, which came into effect in September 1984, produced unintended consequences that in major respects paved the way for the change begun in 1990. They also had a big impact on de Klerk's career.

The first, already touched upon, was Treurnicht's 1982 decision, before the tricameral constitution was enacted into law, to break away and form the Conservative Party. For several years prior to the break Treurnicht had sniped at P. W. Botha's reforms, always backing away at the last moment to avoid a rupture. The proposed tricameral constitution envisaged a limited degree of power sharing across colour lines ('sham consociationalism', its critics called it), to which Treurnicht objected on the ostensible grounds that this violated the principle that each 'group' should have its own government.

The NP's strongly federal character made the provincial leaders important barons and thus De Klerk's election as Transvaal leader of the NP gave him a significant power base. More than this, however, Treurnicht's departure rid the NP of an incubus. As de Klerk put it:

> The departure of the Conservatives greatly facilitated the task of those of us who remained behind. It was no longer necessary to make unwieldy compromises to keep them on board. A ... principle in transformation management is ... the encouragement of those who are steadfastly opposed to change to disembark (de Klerk, 1997a, p. 4).

The open racism of the Conservatives held up a mirror to more reform-minded nationalists, whose numbers were growing, to show them what the NP itself had been like in the not-so-distant past. The image repelled them, and strengthened their wish for further dissociation from that racist past (Willem De Klerk, 1991, p. 109).

A second consequence reinforced the first: in the joint committees and plenary sessions in which all three chambers met, the nationalists learned firsthand from their Coloured and Indian counterparts of the human damage inflicted on their communities by apartheid.[5] Even the relatively moderate politicians of the Coloured and Indian chambers were able to make many nationalists feel a sense of guilt.

A third consequence was the impetus that the tricameral constitution provided for large-scale mobilisation of protest. Large numbers of Coloured and Indian people, supposed beneficiaries of the new system, boycotted the 1984 elections for their respective chambers. The system's exclusion of Africans was regarded not only as an intolerable affront to the majority, but also as a dangerous source of potential instability. The formation of the United Democratic Front (UDF) in 1983, combined with the powerful leverage of the rising trade union movement, represented a challenge to the old order. The UDF, a loose coalition of organisations, swiftly gravitated towards support for the ANC. Heavy-handed coercive action could temporarily curb protest, but effective government became impossible over wide areas of the country. Apart from the precipitate decline in the value of the currency, declining investor confidence slowed the economic growth rate.

It was these domestic factors rather than the relatively minor activities of the ANC's armed wing, *Umkhonto we Sizwe*, that led increasing numbers of nationalists, including de Klerk, to realise that apartheid's days were numbered. No credible African leader would be inveigled into nationalist-sponsored negotiating forums unless they were premised upon the lifting of the bans on the ANC and other organisations and the unconditional release of Nelson Mandela and other imprisoned leaders. Mandela himself had on several occasions refused release unless this were unconditional. For the NP, Mandela posed a dilemma: he was the most famous political prisoner in the world, and his death in prison would have disastrous consequences. On the other hand, releasing him into a political vacuum, in which the ANC remained proscribed, was likely to have serious destabilising consequences. In short, if Mandela were to be released he would have to be released into a process.

By the early 1980s de Klerk was aware that apartheid was failing, and there is evidence that his conscience was troubling him. But whatever his private misgivings, de Klerk remained a loyal member of the Botha government. His relations with Botha were correct, if never cordial. De Klerk was not intimidated[6] and over time he grew steadily more uneasy about Botha's militarist style and the influence of the group of mostly military security advisors, colloquially called 'securocrats', who surrounded him. Increasingly, the State Security Council, an ostensibly advisory body established by Botha to consider security issues, eclipsed the cabinet in influencing decisions, a trend of which the legalistic de Klerk disapproved.

However, de Klerk supported the general direction of Botha's reforms which, he recognised, were undeniably undermining some of apartheid's pillars. But de Klerk also shared Botha's visceral anticommunism. Though he eschewed crude, McCarthyite 'red-baiting', he believed that if the ANC was not communist-controlled then it was at least subject to powerful communist influence through the South African Communist Party. Neighbouring Angola, Mozambique and Zimbabwe had adopted Marxist–Leninist approaches, and Cuban troops fought in Angola. Even if it was far-fetched to conjure up images of the Russian bear at South Africa's borders, there were plausible grounds for supposing that an ANC government would introduce radical socialist measures. The Marxist rhetoric of the ANC and its faithful support of Soviet foreign policy positions – which reflected the ANC's reliance on Soviet material and diplomatic support – provided further grounds (Thomas, 1996, pp. 149–66). It was no coincidence, therefore, that de Klerk's major move of 1990 occurred only after the fall of the Berlin Wall and the general collapse of Marxist–Leninist states in the Eastern bloc.

P. W. Botha's acceptance of South Africa as 'one nation' and his 1987 statement that South Africa had outgrown colonial paternalism and apartheid and that 'there needed to be the sharing of power between its different communities' (South African Institute of Race Relations, 1988, p. 90), further encouraged de Klerk to seek an alternative. The tumult in the towns and cities added urgency to the need for an inclusive settlement.

From the mid 1980s stealthy emissaries from government and other organisations such as the Afrikaner Broederbond (a secret, elitist and influential body) made contact with the ANC. There were also visits to Mandela by several members of the cabinet (see Sparks, 1994). Botha, however, refused either to release Mandela or to lift the ban on the ANC unless they foreswore violence. Since the ANC regarded its capacity to fight a 'war of liberation' as a significant potential bargaining chip in its dealings with the South African government, it rejected Botha's condition. Thus the stalemate intensified. Botha, apart from a visceral dislike of the ANC and its communist allies, was incapable of thinking beyond an apartheid-style paradigm: for him the statutory population groups, laid down by the Population Registration Act of 1950, had to be the building blocks of any new constitutional order.

From 1986 onwards South Africa drifted rudderless. Botha, surrounded by 'securocrats', grew increasingly isolated, not only from his party caucus but also from reality. He suffered a stroke during 1988, news of which was hushed up, and then another major stroke felled him on 18 January 1989. Shortly thereafter Botha announced that the roles of *hoofleier* (leader-in-chief) of the NP and the state presidency were to be separated. The NP caucus thereupon proceeded to elect de Klerk as party leader, by a narrow margin of eight votes.[7]

For all his failings, Botha cleared the decks for de Klerk's great leap forward – a fact which de Klerk always acknowledged. Botha's reforms tore down some of apartheid's main pillars, and his firm statement – however qualified – that 'the peoples of the Republic of South Africa make up one nation' destroyed the 'separate nations' belief that had underpinned apartheid ideology until then. But in the end Botha proved incapable of liberating himself from the old racial paradigm.

President de Klerk

P. W. Botha's illness and de Klerk's election as NP leader early in 1989 initiated a messy period of dyarchy. Relations between the two deteriorated steadily. Finally, at a cabinet meeting on 14 August 1989 the cabinet unanimously pressed Botha into reluctant resignation (Prinsloo, 1997, pp. 390–419). De Klerk was sworn in as acting State President on 15 August, and after the general elections of 6 September he was unanimously elected as State President. Although the CP had made menacing gains, winning over 30 per cent of the white vote, de Klerk derived comfort from his belief that the remaining 70 per cent (including 21 per cent who supported the liberal Democratic Party) had given him a mandate for reform. Little in the NP's campaign, however, had prepared its supporters for the scale of the impending changes.

De Klerk denies that his was a kind of Damascene conversion which occurred only late in 1989. He contends that he took his 'quantum leap' in 1985–86 when the NP abandoned 'separate development', as apartheid was officially called. His speeches, beginning in 1986, did show a consistently reformist line, even when facing ferocious CP opposition in the elections of 1987 and 1989. However another quantum leap was required to move from generalities about power sharing to the acknowledgement that no settlement would be possible without the ANC's inclusion. For the leader of a party that had demonised the ANC for so long, this was the painful nettle that would have to be grasped.

At the same time South Africa's 'democracy' remained a racial oligarchy, with white leaders dependent on continuing white support in elections, elections which provided real enough contests. De Klerk could not be complacent about carrying his support-base with him. In the mid 1980s racial feelings were more polarised than ever before. Crude right-wing racism seemed rampant – the 1987 election showed that some 30 per cent of the white electorate supported right-wing parties. White living standards were dropping by about one per cent per annum, while the tightening noose of sanctions accelerated economic contraction and inflamed white xenophobia, mainly to the benefit of the right wing.

Once elected NP leader in 1989 de Klerk gave a commitment that any fundamental constitutional amendments would be preceded by an election or a referendum. Though reformists fiercely criticised this commitment, de Klerk had realised that – leaving to one side the possibility of a revolution - a paradigm shift could occur only with the consent or acquiescence of a majority of whites. He had surely also realised that would-be reformers in ethnically or racially divided societies ran the risk of being swept aside and replaced by hardliners. So his was a careful balancing act. But it was also at this time that he made the crucial shift away from the idea of 'compulsory' group affiliation, telling a surprised parliament early in 1989 that:

> the NP is not as ideologically obsessed with the group concept as has been suggested by many critics .... Our strong emphasis on group rights, alongside individual rights, is based on the reality of South Africa and not on an ideological obsession or racial prejudice ... my party strives for a non-racialistic country, a country free of racism, of racial hatred ... free of negative discrimination on the basis of race.... Reality dictates recognition of group diversity. How we do it, so as to ensure that it will not be on a discriminatory basis, is the challenge we face. (House of Assembly Debates, 1989, cols 201–2).

How ripe were whites for fundamental change? Attitudes were polarising rapidly: the growth of the right wing owed much to deteriorating living standards and political apprehensiveness; but on the other hand the rise in support for the DP and the continuing disaffection of Afrikaner elites showed readiness for change. Also of considerable significance was the influence of the Afrikaner Broederbond, whose approximately 17 000 members occupied many key positions in the state, the party, the church, the professions and the economy. The Broederbond's principal function was to further Afrikaner cultural interests, but it also served as a think-tank and a two-way channel of communication between leaders in all spheres of society and their followers.

In the 1980s the Broederbond became a powerful force for reform that helped pave the way for de Klerk's initiatives. Its reform proposals were contained in a document entitled 'Basic Constitutional Preconditions for the Continued Existence of the Afrikaner' (*Afrikaner Basiese Staatkundige Voorwaardes vir die Voortbestaan van die*), which was approved by the Broederbond's executive committee in November 1986. The document was premised on the view that 'The greatest risk that we run today is not to take risks. If the Afrikaner cannot reach a negotiated settlement, it is inevitable that structures in which he will have no say will be forced upon him' (Die Afrikanerbond, 1997, p. 21).[8]

In forcing the pace of change in 1990 and afterwards de Klerk maintained that he was doing no more than carrying through to their logical conclusion policy changes adopted by the NP in 1985–86; power sharing in an undivided South Africa had been accepted. It was now a question of removing obstacles to the negotiating process and developing appropriate models for a democratic constitution. In invoking this logic de Klerk was revealing another characteristic feature of his mental make-up: he was *konsekwent*; (consistent).[9] From the time de Klerk decided to launch his initiative he never doubted that he had done the right thing, a state of mind that was to give him self-assurance during the tough battles that marked the transition.

Opting for the *status quo*, whilst it remained a theoretical possibility, would have been an increasingly uncomfortable choice because of the steadily tightening noose of international isolation. Commentators continue to disagree about the impact of sanctions – both public and private – in inducing change in South Africa. Critics point to the fact that the economy was in bad shape well before economic pressures first began to be applied. What is beyond dispute is that such pressures made a bad situation worse. F. W. de Klerk himself made this point abundantly clear during the 1989 election campaign: South Africa, he argued, had to restore its traditional links with Western trading partners and investors if the country was to emerge from its deepening economic crisis. Real doubts were emerging in business and political cycles about the country's political stability. Above all, sanctions, however haphazardly applied, had by the late 1980s contributed to the creation of a siege mentality. De Klerk saw clearly that economic recovery would depend on political reform.

If tightening sanctions acted as a growing negative incentive, de Klerk's reformist hand was also positively strengthened by the unfolding Gorbachev reforms in the Soviet Union and, in particular, by the fall in November 1989 of the Berlin Wall. As he later described matters, 'It was if God had taken a hand – a new turn in world history.... We had to seize the opportunity' (Waldmeir, 1997, pp. 136-7). In the southern African context, this had a particular significance for the long drawn-out dispute between the South African Republic and the United Nations over the status of Namibia. The Namibian/Angolan peace initiative, which included the gradual withdrawal of Cuban troops, provided a major incentive for de Klerk's dramatic change of course. The Soviet Union could no longer be perceived as engaging in a 'total onslaught' against the Republic. The USSR's support for the Namibian settlement and its unwillingness to continue as the exiled ANC's long-established patron gave de Klerk a vital degree of flexibility in dealing with white domestic opinion in South Africa. Right-wing Afrikaner nationalists were, in particular, effectively disarmed; no longer could they point to the Soviet Union as a significant threat to South Africa.

De Klerk's eagerness to move rapidly was spurred by reports to the cabinet of a deteriorating security situation. The 1980s had been a turbulent decade: internal violence was extensive, as masses of blacks mobilised to protest and the ANC's armed wing, *Umkhonto we Sizwe* (the Spear of the Nation), stepped up its campaign of guerrilla war. Niel Barnard, Director of the National Intelligence Service and a key actor in making contact with Mandela and other ANC leaders, pulled no punches in urging the government to get on with democratisation: the whites otherwise had no future. Now was the time to begin, Barnard insisted, before the whites' position had eroded and their bargaining resources for negotiations had dwindled. Years later, de Klerk told an NP congress that the NP 'could have clung to power for another five to ten years but had relinquished power out of conviction'. The NP had 'all the powerful instruments in its hands, and could have continued to escape the pressures of economic isolation'. The ANC 'was not winning the bush war. We have not been pushed into this change – we led it. We did what we did on the basis of inner conviction' (de Klerk, 1994.

But the truth was that, as de Klerk told parliament in 1991, South Africa was falling into an 'absolute impasse' (House of Assembly Debates, 2 May 1991, col. 7272). Nelson Mandela had reached the same conclusion even earlier, in 1985:

> We had been fighting against white minority rule for three-quarters of a century. We had been engaged in the armed struggle for more than two decades. Many people on both sides had died. The enemy was strong and resolute. Yet even with all their bombers and tanks, they must have sensed they were on the wrong side of history. We had right on our side, but not yet might. It was clear to me that a military victory was a distant if not impossible dream. It simply did not make sense for both sides to lose thousands if not millions of lives in a conflict that was unnecessary. They must have known this as well. It was time to talk (Mandela, 1994, p. 513).

It was a rare historic moment in which antagonistic yet somehow symbiotic leaderships recognised that a deadlock existed and that the conflict could be continued only at appalling cost. De Klerk and Mandela began the process of negotiation with very different political and constitutional aims in mind, but both realised that neither could succeed without the other. Between 1990 and 1994 relations between the two were often strained, sometimes close to the point of rupture, but they survived and the negotiating process was kept on track. As Mandela later said: 'I never sought to undermine Mr de Klerk, for the practical reason that the weaker he was, the weaker the negotiating process. To make peace with an enemy, one must work with that enemy, and that enemy becomes your partner' (ibid, p. 604).

Leading the transition

From the onset de Klerk realised that he could not succeed unless his political base remained secure. The process that began on 2 February 1990, he said:

was rather like paddling a canoe into a long stretch of dangerous rapids. You may start the process and determine the initial direction. However, after that the canoe is seized by enormous and often uncontrollable forces. All that the canoeist can do is to maintain his balance, avoid the rocks and steer as best he can – and right the canoe if it capsizes. It is a time for cool heads and firm, decisive action (de Klerk, 1997a, p. 3).

De Klerk's cabinet and caucus remained firmly behind him. It was a remarkable feature of the four-year process of transition, which culminated in the inclusive election of April 1994, that not a single member of either cabinet or caucus defected. All four provincial NP leaders were solidly behind de Klerk, and it was only the less influential cabinet ministers who occasionally expressed reservations. The truth was that once the canoe was into the rapids there was no alternative but to go forward – and to try to stay afloat.

The white electorate, however, remained a source of concern. Business and the white middle class in general supported change, but there were ominous rumblings from the right wing, including the Conservative Party and a growing number of extraparliamentary organisations, some with a proclivity for violence. Throughout 1991 by-elections showed a political tide that was turning against the NP. The trend reached a climax on 19 February 1992 when the hitherto safe NP seat of Potchefstroom fell to a rampant CP. The NP had thrown everything it had into the contest and still lost, and de Klerk concluded that he had 'no more moral basis' for continuing the negotiating process.

In an act of political daring and courage, de Klerk decided to go for broke by calling a snap referendum in which white voters would be asked to express an opinion on whether the reform process should continue. Although he discussed the referendum option with a senior colleague, he unilaterally fixed the date for 17 March 1991, and subsequently revealed that his caucus would almost certainly have rejected his decision had it been broached with them beforehand (de Klerk, 1997b). De Klerk expected to win 55 per cent of the votes, which would have been something of a pyrrhic victory. The actual outcome, a 68.7 per cent vote for continuing the process, surprised most people and gave de Klerk the mandate he needed. It was a key development.[10]

How was so thumping a victory to be explained? The options facing South Africa's whites were stark: either the negotiating process, with all its uncertainties and risks, continued, or the country would slide into civil war. For the right wingers de Klerk's step into uncharted waters threw up numerous opportunities for racists to exploit, but the alternatives they offered were bankrupt: a return to the full rigour of apartheid, long advocated by the CP, was unthinkable; and the quest for a white-controlled enclave, a so-called *volkstaat*, was a chimera. De Klerk had successfully called the right wing's bluff. If de Klerk's base among whites was secure, he also enjoyed considerable popularity among non-whites. Nearly all fully supported his initiatives and, according to polls, 80 per cent of urban Africans expressed satisfaction with his leadership, some even ranking him higher than Mandela (*Economist*, 29 February 1992). Right-wing opposition, however, did not fade. On the contrary, some of it was to assume more sinister and violent forms that could yet derail the transition.

De Klerk and the constitutional issue

In a speech on 21 January 1997 in London, de Klerk reviewed the outcome of the tortuous negotiations that had led to agreement on an interim constitution at the end of 1993 and – eventually, after the intervening elections of April 1994 – to acceptance of the final constitution on 8 May 1996:

> The decision to surrender the right to national sovereignty is certainly one of the most painful that any leader or people can ever be asked to take. Indeed, the maintenance of national sovereignty, of a people's right to rule themselves, is regarded in most countries as non-negotiable. Most nations would be prepared to risk total war and catastrophe rather than to surrender this right. Yet this was the decision we had to take (de Klerk, 1997a, p. 3).

The speech caused a stir in South Africa. Even newspapers sympathetic to the NP accused it of having sold the pass in the constitutional negotiations. *Die Burger*, for example, questioned whether he would have obtained a mandate to proceed had he made the speech during the negotiations because 'he asked for a mandate for power-sharing, not for surrender' (*Die Burger*, 6 February 1997).

It is certainly true that de Klerk and his negotiators ended up with less than they had originally sought. The question is, however, whether they could realistically have expected more. At the core of the NP's proposals was a scheme for power sharing: a multiparty presidency, consisting of the leader of the three biggest parties in the First

House, would, by consensus, appoint ministers who would constitute a multiparty cabinet. The chairmanship of the presidency would rotate on an annual basis; the Second House would represent federal regions on an equal basis and parties who received a certain minimum level of support in a particular region would be given equal representation in that region's Second House representation.

The proposals, which were said to be modelled on Switzerland's political system, were scorned by much of the opposition, including the ANC, as an attempt to smuggle a white veto into the new constitution – which de Klerk denied. The NP's proposals would almost certainly have been unworkable in practice. It is also likely that they represented an opening bid and would have to be modified in the course of negotiations. Nevertheless they at least pointed to the difficult problem of sustaining democracy in deeply divided societies: how is group domination or the tyranny of the majority to be avoided?[11]

A limited degree of power sharing was agreed in the interim constitution: each party winning 20 or more seats in the 400–strong National Assembly was entitled to one or more cabinet portfolios in proportion to the number of seats held by it relative to the number of seats held by other parties; in addition every party winning 80 or more seats was entitled to nominate an executive deputy president. Cabinet decisions in this Government of National Unity (GNU) were to be taken by consensus, though subject to 'the need for effective government' (Clause 89(2) of the (Interim) Constitution of the Republic of South Africa – Act 200 of 1997) This power-sharing arrangement was to last until 1999 – the final constitution scrapped the concept.

The ANC acquiesced in the GNU less out of conviction than a pragmatic wish to ease the NP's acceptance of majority rule and defuse any possible counterrevolutionary activity on the part of an enemy that had not been defeated and remained powerful (Welsh, 1994b, pp. 25–6).

The NP's harvest was similarly meagre when it came to its demand for decentralisation in a federal state. The ANC was hostile to federalism for several reasons: it could be a way of reinstating discredited 'homelands' in a new, democratic guise; it could be a launch-pad for secessionist movements – in particular they feared the Inkatha Freedom Party's potential secessionist drive in its stronghold, KwaZulu-Natal; and federalism could provide wealthier provinces with a means of resisting moves to redistribute wealth to poorer provinces. Above all the ANC was a liberation movement which favoured 'democratic centralism' in its own ranks and a unitary system for the state which it would shortly govern (Ottaway, 1991, p. 69). At most the ANC would concede some measure of decentralisation of administrative functions.

The final constitution suggests that the ANC largely got its way. Provincial powers were strictly limited. At most the constitution could be described as unitary with federal figleaves. De Klerk and his chief negotiator, Roelf Meyer (minister of constitutional development in de Klerk's cabinet), denied that the NP had capitulated. They pointed out that the NP had successfully resisted the ANC's demands for a virtual takeover of power – the institution of a non-elected interim government that would rule by decree and oversee the election of a constituent assembly that would draft a new constitution. This proposed procedure offended de Klerk's legal punctiliousness because it implied interim rule in a constitutional vacuum. De Klerk insisted on constitutional continuity: hence the multistage process that led to adoption of the final constitution.

De Klerk acknowledged that the NP was disappointed with the quasi-federal aspect of the constitution, but could point to other features which, he claimed, resulted from NP bargaining: basic rights for mother-tongue education (one of Afrikaner nationalism's historical demands), a 'relatively good Bill of Rights', separation of the powers and the principle of a constitutional state, all of which were designed to strengthen pluralism (de Klerk, 1997c). Meyer goes further, acknowledging implicitly that the NP had shifted from earlier positions to more flexible ones. Thus:

> Success would not be found in an over-emphasised, unworkable federalism, a veto right for minorities against government decisions and an excessive entrenchment of power-sharing.... Given the political realities of South Africa, the NP realised that it would be far more functional to entrench minority rights on an individual basis (Meyer, 1997).

The course of negotiating situations roughly reflects the strengths of the respective parties. If South Africa's negotiations initially reflected an approximate parity of political resources between the ANC and the NP, that changed over time. The Convention for a Democratic South Africa (CODESA) broke down in May 1992 and was followed by a bleak 'winter of discontent', in which de Klerk and Mandela fired verbal salvoes at each other and civil war seemed a real possibility. Systematic use of 'rolling mass action' (marches, protest demonstrations and strikes) by the ANC raised the political temperature even higher and accelerated the downward spiral of the economy. What the ANC in fact demonstrated was that it could hold the country to ransom – and the NP government could do little about it. The consequence was a decided lurch away from parity of bargaining resources to a new situation in which the ANC was dominant: from now on it would call the shots.

Later occurrences further weakened the NP's bargaining position. First came the 10 April 1993 assassination of Chris Hani, the SACP leader (and a strong contender to succeed Mandela), by a right-winger. The country again trembled on the brink as waves of anger dashed against the white government. Mandela had to use all of his immense moral authority to calm the situation. After this it was clear that the NP's days of effective rule were numbered. Hani's killing foreshortened the period of transition in that the ANC now demanded that the date for the first democratic election be fixed, as a stratagem for placating the angry masses. The NP, under duress, agreed to 27 April 1994.

The second factor was the election itself, which, although allegedly marred by serious irregularities, gave the ANC a huge victory, with nearly 63 per cent of the vote. The NP trailed badly, winning 20 per cent where it had hoped to win up to 35 per cent of the vote which, together with the votes won by smaller parties, might have resulted in a less commanding position for the ANC in the final round of constitutional negotiations. These negotiations took place in the Constitutional Assembly, which was the Parliament sitting in a constitution-making capacity. Although decisions, including the adoption of the final draft, required a two-thirds majority, the ANC's preponderance meant that it got its way on most issues.

Could the NP have obtained a better deal? Were its negotiators out manoeuvred by their ANC counterparts? As far as the latter question is concerned, the NP learned to its cost at CODESA that the ANC team was able, thoroughly well-prepared and tough. It is highly doubtful that stronger safeguards for minorities could have been obtained. It is also the case that constitutional provisions, while by no means unimportant, are less effective safeguards then a political culture that is tolerant of minorities. No government of South Africa can afford to alienate the whites, given their numbers and their economic power. That consideration is likely to be their best hope that majority rule will be tempered by consideration for minorities. De Klerk, it seems, recognised this.

Leadership qualities face their sternest test in times of adversity. De Klerk's finest hour may have been his decision to call a high-risk referendum in February 1992; but his recognition, when the scales had tipped against him, that the most important consideration was to sustain the momentum of the negotiating process and to avert another dangerous breakdown, was also powerful testimony to his mettle and his commitment to the cause of constitutional reform.

De Klerk's legacy

Early in May 1994 de Klerk graciously conceded defeat to Mandela's ANC and assumed his post as executive deputy-president in the Government of National Unity. The device of a Government of National Unity succeeded as a transitional mechanism to the extent that it helped to lower the stakes of this founding election: had the election been contested on a 'winner-take-all' basis it is quite possible that the serious violence in the run-up to the election would have continued.

De Klerk withdrew the NP from the cabinet in mid-1996 and became leader of the Opposition until he retired from politics in September 1997. The preceding year had been a difficult time for him and his party. Not only was he beset by personal problems and hurt by what he clearly felt was a witch-hunt being conducted against him by the Truth and Reconciliation Commission, but also the NP was still experiencing difficulty in adjusting to its new role in opposition.

In his short farewell speech to parliament on 9 September 1997, delivered amidst a hubbub of barracking from ANC backbenchers, de Klerk recalled that it was from the same podium that he had announced the lifting of the ban on the ANC and the release of Mandela:

> The past cannot be undone. The future presents tremendous challenges. It is time to end sterile debates and degrading and divisive reproaches about the past. It is time to focus all our energy and resources on the solution of the problems of today and tomorrow (authors' archive).

De Klerk had come a long way in a short time. Given his background, it was inevitable that a strong sense of Afrikaner identity, including a firm commitment to apartheid, was woven into his very persona. In his earlier apologies de Klerk would insist that apartheid was a policy espoused by him in good faith, which had gone horribly wrong. Before the Truth and Reconciliation Commission, however, de Klerk went further than ever before:

> Let me place once and for all a renewed apology on record. Apartheid was wrong.... This renewed apology is offered in a spirit of true repentance, in full knowledge of the tremendous harm that apartheid has done to millions of South Africans (de Klerk, 1996).[12]

De Klerk's legacy can perhaps best be measured by considering two alternative scenarios. First, what might have happened if Botha had not fallen ill in 1989? Although he was already 73 he may well have wanted to remain in office at least until 1992, and perhaps even longer. The years of rudderless drift of the mid-1980s suggest that Botha lacked the will and/or the creativity to extricate the white minority from its deteriorating position. Nothing in his record suggests that he would have acquired these qualities or that he would have been prepared to moderate his defiant attitude.

Second, what might have happened had Barend du Plessis won the election for the party leadership and ultimately acceded to the presidency? His premature retirement from politics in 1992, apparently as a result of nervous exhaustion, suggests that he might not have had the toughness and resilience that the transition negotiations demanded of all participants. But du Plessis, who fully supported de Klerk's subsequent initiative, has acknowledged other reasons why he would have been unlikely to achieve what de Klerk was able to do:

> If I had won, I would have had to drag him [de Klerk] and his whole *verkrampte* [reactionary] outfit screaming and clawing to the other side, and that would have taken years and we would have lost opportunities.... But de Klerk could take this conservative bunch with him, in a very short period consolidate the caucus, and from that power base, he could move. And precisely because he had been a *verkrampte*, he could convince the electorate. He could say to people, 'I've been in the old system and it failed'.... So he could justify a quantum leap to the populace more easily (Waldmeir, 1997, p. 112).

Jack Spence has argued that de Klerk

bears comparison with right wing leaders such as Charles de Gaulle and Richard Nixon. Unencumbered by ideological baggage of a narrowly restricting kind, both were able to display a masterly understanding of what had to be done in difficult circumstances and were, in any case, more interested in the exercise of power and the imperatives of national survival than in grandiose objectives of a millenial kind (Spence, 1994, p. 5).

De Klerk's achievement ranks high on the scale of comparable achievements by other modern political leaders. He would be the first to recognise that this was built on the openings created by the tentative reforms of his predecessor, and that he benefited from a conjunction of more or less propitious circumstances. But as Geldenhuys has argued, such extraneous influences as international pressure and the collapse of the Soviet threat, important though they undoubtedly were, 'would probably not have led to the demise of apartheid at that time and in that particular fashion' (Geldenhuys, 1998, p. 80). F. W. de Klerk's lucid moral and political analysis led him to believe that the transition process had to be taken to its logical conclusion. As he simply put it, 'We could not go on the way we did before. No matter how difficult things may be now, they would have been far worse had we not made the change we did' (cited in Johnson, 1997), and it was his strategic and political skills which facilitated the realisation of that aim. It was a rare feat for a minority to yield power to a majority that was, moreover, racially and culturally alien. The least that can be said about de Klerk's statesmanship is that he was part of a series of elements which, whilst insufficient in themselves to bring about peaceful transition, were vitally necessary. Together with his fellow Nobel Peace Prize winner, Nelson Mandela, he demonstrated that having the right leader in the right place at the right time can make a difference to the outcome of events.

F. W. de Klerk: chronology

1936, 18 March:	Born in Johannesburg to a highly political Afrikaner Nationalist family (his father was a cabinet minister and president of the Senate). The family were devout members of the Reformed (*Dopper*) Church.
1958	Graduated in law with distinction from the Potchefstroom University of Christian Higher Education, where he became actively involved in National Party politics.
1961–72	Law practice in the Transvaal town of Vereeniging.
1972	Elected in a by-election to the House of Assembly.

1975	Information officer for the Transvaal National Party.
1978	Appointed minister of posts and telecommunications and minister of social welfare and pensions.
1979–80	Minister of posts and telecommunications and minister of sport and recreation.
1980–82	Minister of mineral and energy affairs.
1982	Dr Andries Treurnicht resigned as Transvaal leader of the National Party and broke away to form the Liberal Party.
1982–89	De Klerk subsequently elected Transvaal leader of the National Party.
1982–85	Minister of internal affairs.
1984 September	P. W. Botha's tricameral constitution came into effect.
1984–89	Minister of national education and planning.
1989	Botha suffered a stroke and resigned first as National Party leader and then as state president.
1989	De Klerk became leader of the National Party and from August to September was acting state president of South Africa.
1989–94	Elected state president of South Africa, beating his main rival Barend du Plessis by just nine votes.
1990, 2 February	De Klerk announced release of Mandela and the lifting of the ban on the ANC and other proscribed organisations.
1990–96	Frequently fraught constitutional negotiations ultimately led to a fully democratic constitution.
1992, February	National Party lost safe seat of Potchefstroom in by-election.
1992, 17 March	De Klerk won go-for-broke referendum on continuing the negotiating process.
1993, 10 April	Chris Hani assassinated.
1993	De Klerk shared Nobel Peace Prize with Nelson Mandela.
1994–96	Executive deputy president in Government of National Unity.
1994, 27 April	First all-South Africa democratic elections under transitional regime: the ANC won 63 per cent and the National Party 20 per cent of the votes. The ANC thereafter became far more assertive and authoritative in the ongoing constitutional negotiations.
1996, 8 May	New constitution accepted.
1996, June	De Klerk withdrew National Party from governing coalition and became leader of the opposition.
1997, 26 August	De Klerk retired as leader of the National Party and retired from politics.

Notes

1   The authors would like to thank Dawie de Villiers, Hernus Kriel, Leon Wessels, Piet Marais (all of whom served in F. W. de Klerk's Cabinet), Dave Steward (former director-general in the state president's office), Colin Eglin and Ken Andrew for assistance in providing information for and criticism of this chapter. Thanks also to Catherine Welsh and Virginia van der Vliet.

Above all, thanks are expressed to F. W. de Klerk himself for patiently submitting to several interviews.

2   Although de Klerk learned to speak and write fluent English, there is no evidence of friendships with English-speaking whites, let alone with blacks.

3   He was, however, critical of aspects of apartheid's implementation (for example the NP's refusal to implement the developmental proposals for the African 'homelands' made by the 1955 Tomlinson Commission, whose brief it had been to examine the economic viability of apartheid).

4   'Incorrectly, I gained an ultra-conservative image. I never formed part of a political school of thought, and I deliberately kept out of the cliques and foments [sic] of the enlightened and conservative factions of the party. If the policy I propounded was ultra-conservative, then that was the policy; it was not necessarily I who was ultra-conservative. I saw my role as that of an interpreter of the party's real median policy at any stage' (F. W. de Klerk, cited in Willem de Klerk, 1991, p. 24).

5   The Group Areas Act, for example, which provided for forced residential and business segregation, meant hardship and misery for those victims who were forced to leave their homes.

6   Botha was an irascible man with a volcanic temper, and he was said to be capable of reducing cabinet members to tears; his revealing nickname was *Die Groot Krokodil* – the Big Crocodile.

7   His closest rival, Barend du Plessis, the personable minister of finance, was assumed to be more strongly reformist than de Klerk, who was supported by most of the conservatives. Du Plessis, moreover, was said to have been the favoured candidate of the 'securocrat' element in the caucus.

8   That the Afrikaner power elite was ripe for change was indicated by the fact that 89 per cent of the Broederbrond's branches and 86 per cent of its individual members indicated that they agreed with the general thrust of the document (Die Afrikanerbond, 1997).

9   The literal translation of this word is 'consistent', but the Afrikaans word carries a moral connotation of steadfastness.

10   It also conveniently circumvented another potential hazard, in the form of the commitment de Klerk had made in 1989 that any fundamental constitutional change would be preceded by an election or a referendum requesting a mandate for such a change.

11   As Vernon Bogdanor (1997, p. 66) has observed, 'divided societies that have attained stability have all adopted a model of government whose essence is the sharing of power'.

12   De Klerk went on: 'I apologise in my capacity as leader of the National Party to the millions of South Africans who suffered the wrenching disruption of forced removals in respect of their homes, businesses and land. Who over the years suffered the shame of being arrested for pass law offences. Who over the decades and indeed centuries suffered the indignities and humiliation of racial discrimination. Who for a long time were prevented from exercising their full democratic rights in the land of their birth. Who were unable to achieve their full potential because of job reservation. And who in any other way suffered as a result of discriminatory legislation and policies' (de Klerk, 1996).

References

Adam, Heribert and Kogila, Moodley (1993) *The Negotiated Revolution : Society and Politics in Post-Apartheid South Africa*, (Johannesburg: Jonathan Ball).

Asmal, Kadar, Louise Asmal and Ronald Suresh Roberts (1996), *Reconciliation Through Truth: A Reckoning of Apartheid's Criminal Governance* (Cape Town: David Philip).

Bogdanor, Vernon (1997) 'Forms of Autonomy and the Protection of Minorities', *Daedalus*, vol 126, no. 2.

de Klerk, F. W. (1986a) interview in *Focus Letter*, Helen Suzman Foundation, October.

de Klerk, F. W. (1994) interview in *Argus*, Cape Town, 17 November.

de Klerk, F. W. (1996) submission to the Truth and Reconciliation Commission and Transcript of Public Hearing, 21 August.

de Klerk, F. W. (1997a) speech to the partners of Andersen Consulting, London, 21 January.

de Klerk, F. W. (1997b) interview in *Die Burger*, 6 February.

de Klerk, F. W. (1997c) interview in *Rapport*, Johannesburg, 9 February.

de Klerk, F. W. (1999) *The Last Trek: A New Beginning* (London: Macmillan).

de Klerk, Willem (1991) *F.W. de Klerk: The Man in his Time* (Johannesburg: Ball).

Die Afrikanerbond (1997) *Draer van 'n Ideaal: 1918-1997* (Johannesburg: Die Afrikanerbond).

Ellis, Stephen and Tsepo, Sechaba (1992) *Comrades Against Apartheid: The ANC and the South African Communist Party in Exile* (London: James Currey).

Geldenhuys, Deon (1998) *Foreign Political Engagement – Remaking States in the Post-Cold War World* (Basingstoke: Macmillan).

Hexam, Irving (1981) *The Irony of Apartheid: The Struggle for National Independence of Afrikaner Calvinism against British Imperialism* (New York: Edward Mellen Press)

Innes, Duncan (1989) 'Multinational Companies and Disinvestment', in Mark Orkin (ed.) *Sanctions Against Apartheid* (Cape Town and Johannesburg: Catholic Institute of International Relations).

Institute for Black Research (1993) *The Codesa File: Negotiating a Non-Racial Democracy in South Africa* (Durban: Madiba).

Johnson, R. W. (1997) 'The man South Africans could never quite forgive', *The Times*, 27 August.

Kotzé, Hennie, and Deon Geldenhuys (1990) 'Damascus Road', in *Leadership* no. 9.

Mandela, Nelson (1992) letter to F. W. de Klerk (text released by the ANC), 26 June.

Mandela, Nelson (1994) *Long Walk to Freedom: The Autobiography of Nelson Mandela* (London: Little, Brown).

Menzies, Robert (1967) *Afternoon Light: Some Memories of Men and Events* (London: Cassell).

Meyer, Roelf (1997) interview in *Die Burger*, 20 February.

Mitchell, John (ed.) (1998) *Companies in a World of Conflict* (London: Earth Scan Publications for the Royal Institute of International Affairs).

Oppenheimer, H. F. (1986) *Biennial Report of the National Chairman* (London:

Occasional Paper, (Cape Town and Johannesburg: The South African Institute of International Relations).

Orkin, Mark (ed.) (1989) *Sanctions Against Apartheid* Cape Town and Johannesburg: Catholic Institute of International Relations).

Ottaway, Marina (1991) 'Liberation Movements and Transition to Democracy', *Journal of Modern African Studies*, vol. 29, no. 1

Pottinger, Brian (1988) *The Imperial Presidency: P.W. Botha – the First Ten Years* (Johannesburg: Southern Book Publishers).

Prinsloo, Daan (1997) *Stem uit die Wildenris: 'n Biografie oor oud-press. P W Botha* (Mossel Bay: Vaandel).

Seegers, Annette (1996) *The Military in the Making of Modern South Africa* (London: Tauris Academic Studies).

South African Institute of Race Relations (1988) *Annual Survey of Race Relations for 1987* (Johannesburg: South African Institute of Race Relations).

Sparks, Allister (1994) *Tomorrow is Another Country: The Inside Story of South Africa's Negotiated Revolution* (South Africa: Sandton).

Spence, Jack (ed.) (1994) *Change in South Africa* (London: Pinter for the Royal Institute of International Affairs).

Spence, Jack (1998) 'South Africa: A Case Study in Human Rights and Sanctions', in John Mitchell (ed.), *Companies in a World of Conflict* (London: Earth Scan Publications for the Royal Institute of International Affairs).

Thomas, Scott (1996) *The Diplomacy of Liberation: The Foreign Relations of the ANC Since 1960* (London: Tauris Academic Studies).

Van Dijk, Evert (1991) *FW sê sy sê . . .: Aanhalings uit F.W. de Klerk se Toesprake in die Parliament* (Cape Town: Vlaeberg).

Van Zyl Slabbert, F. (1997) 'FW: Uitverwkoping of uitoorlê?', *Insig*, March.

Waldmeir, Patti (1997) *The Anatomy of a Miracle: The End of Apartheid and the Birth of the New South Africa* (London: Viking).

Welsh, David (1994a) 'The Executive and the African Population', in Robert Schrire (ed.), *Leadership in the Apartheid State: From Malan to de Klerk* (London: Hurst).

Welsh, David (1994b) 'Negotiating a Democratic Constitution', in J. E. Spence (ed.), *Change in South Africa* (London: Pinter for the Royal Institute of International Affairs).

Welsh, David (1995) 'Rightwing Terrorism in South Africa', in *Terrorism and Political Violence*, vol. 7 (Spring).

Wessels, Leon (1994) *Die Einde van 'n Era* (Cape Town: Tafelberg).

Achille Occhetto

*In periods of great transformation it is only possible to span the old
and the new, considering that the changes are born within the old*
(Occhetto, 1994, p. 73)

12 November 1989: the speech that shook the Italian political world, Achille
Occhetto announces his intention to transform the Italian Communist Party.
(*Courtesy of Umberto Gaggioli*)

3
Achille Occhetto: Democratic Explorer
Martin Bull

> *In periods of great transformation it is only possible to span the old and the new, considering that the changes are born within the old*
> (Occhetto, 1994, p. 73)

Shortly after 7 pm on Sunday 3 February 1991, at the Italian Communist Party's headquarters (Botteghe oscure), the red flag bearing the hammer and sickle was lowered for the last time and the new flag of the Democratic Party of the Left (PDS), with its symbol of an oak tree (with a small hammer and sickle on its trunk), was raised in its place. This otherwise routine act was the symbolic completion of an extraordinary transformation of a party born in 1921 as a product of the Russian Revolution. In the space of fifteen months the Italian Communist Party (PCI), the largest communist party in the west, had been dissolved and replaced by a new non-communist party of the left, and it can be largely ascribed to the work of one man: Achille Occhetto.

Yet this remarkable achievement – in a party characterised, like all communist parties, by deep conservatism about fundamental internal reform – was not without its costs for the man himself. Indeed, if Achille Occhetto ever contemplates the relevance of Marxism today, one axiom he is sure not to question is that men make their own history but not in the manner of their own choosing. He might, when looking at the current political situation in Italy (with the former communists in power), be justified in feeling bitter towards a party whose fortunes owe a good deal to him, but from which he felt obliged to resign after a devastating electoral defeat and from which he was then effectively sidelined. The party subsequently enacted a further transformation of Occhetto's own creation, and he is commonly (and unfairly) regarded as a man motivated by little more than personal animosity in his criticisms of the current leader, Massimo D'Alema. In fact Occhetto himself has noted that it is almost impossible for him to make any criticism of the party line now without it being interpreted as bitterness about his own personal fate. For Occhetto is an excellent example of the problems facing any leader of a transition. The very changes generated can undermine the leader's power base, and the benefits of the transition may not come immediately. Consequently, as the transition phase either progresses or begins to close, it can take its leader with it.

In Occhetto's case, however, this was not inevitable. Indeed, the paradox of his fate is that a cursory glance at what happened, suggests that his original objectives in initiating a transformation of the PCI have all been met. Five days after the collapse of the Berlin Wall in October 1989, Occhetto shocked the political world by announcing his intention to transform the PCI into a non-communist party of the left. The effective social democratisation of the PCI had three inter-related objectives: the ending of the so-called 'communist question' in Italy; the subsequent unblocking of the party system which – because of the permanent exclusion of the second largest party from power – had resulted in fifty years of rule of the largest party, Christian Democracy (DC), with its allies, and thus no alternation in government; and the victory of a left-wing coalition led by the newly transformed PCI. By April 1996 all three objectives had been achieved: the old PCI had gone and the 'communist question' was no longer a real issue; the party system was unblocked quite dramatically through the organisational and electoral collapse of both the DC and the Italian Socialist Party (PSI), leading to a transformation of the party system and the possibility of alternation in government; and finally, a centre-left coalition, with the PDS as its principal component, was victorious in the April 1996 elections and subsequently became the main party of government. Yet Occhetto had been effectively constrained into resigning two years earlier, in the spring of 1994. Moreover the PDS was formally dissolved in January 1997 and a new party (Democrats of the Left) was formed one year later, principally because of the perceived failure of the PDS to unite the political left into a single party. This chapter attempts to explain the demise of the man and his party.

Political context

It is impossible to understand the fate of Occhetto and the PDS outside the broader context of postwar Italian politics. In the late 1940s the nascent republic was irrevocably affected by the development of the Cold War (Ginsborg, 1990, chs 2–3). The presence in Italy of the largest communist party in the West ensured a rapid polarisation of political forces and moves on the part of anticommunist parties to keep the PCI out of power. The victory of the DC in the 1948 elections laid the foundations for a particular type of rule over a fifty-year period. This was chiefly characterised by two factors. The first was the operation of the *conventio ad excludendum* (exclusion convention), by which the other parties agreed to exclude the PCI from power because it was an 'anti-system' party. Since the PCI was the second largest party it meant that the DC governed indefinitely in coalition with a marginally varying pattern of coalition partners: there was no alternation in government, only 'peripheral turnover'. The second factor was the consolidation of power by the DC through the politicisation of state structures and the development of patronage policies from the 1950s onwards, policies which eventually degenerated into explicit forms of corruption. This enabled the party effectively to 'buy votes', particularly in the south, and this, combined with virulent anticommunist propaganda, helped ensure the party's long-term survival in office (Pasquino, 1980).

The PCI was never able to overcome its delegitimisation and the 'exclusion convention' remained intact. There were two explanations for this. The first was that, despite the party undergoing considerable changes between the 1940s and the 1980s, its identity remained ambivalent. On the one hand the PCI made its commitment to a parliamentary road unequivocal, it committed itself to upholding the rights and freedoms associated with western democracy, it became increasingly critical of the Soviet Union (and finally broke the umbilical cord with the Soviet motherland over intervention in Poland in 1981), internal debate became gradually more open and the party actually entered the governing 'arena' in the 1970s (by allowing, through its abstention, a minority DC government to carry out certain policies in a period of real crisis, an arrangement which had longer-term implications for the legitimisation of the PCI, which never materialised).

Yet, on the other hand, these steps were never taken to their logical conclusion in terms of the complete social democratisation of the party. Indeed the party was still governed by the Leninist principle of democratic centralism, it remained teleological in nature (aspiring to a goal of 'going beyond' capitalism) and it continued to insist that it remained 'different' from the other political parties. This *diversità* (distinctiveness) was rooted in a commitment to a 'third way' to socialism (between Leninism on the one hand and social democracy on the other), a commitment which was never formally renounced. This ambivalence suited the party leadership internally because it was deeply divided between those who felt that the party should accelerate its social democratisation and those for whom the very word was an anathema (Bull, 1991a).

The second reason lay in the attitudes of the other parties. It became increasingly clear that the 'exclusion convention', no matter how genuine in its origins, was a useful instrument for holding on to power and sharing the benefits of patronage, no matter what progress the PCI made in the direction of social democratisation. The hostile attitude towards the PCI of the PSI under its leader, Bettino Craxi, in the 1980s was exemplary of this attitude. Here was a party which claimed to embody social democracy but which, in reality, had simply become absorbed into the DC's party-regime and was dependent for its survival on clientelistic and corrupt practices.

The effects of this situation were threefold. First, in relation to the political system, Italy developed a peculiar model of democracy. In the absence of alternation in government the state effectively became a huge patronage machine – bloated, costly and inefficient and with vested interests against its reform. Indeed the so-called 'spoils system' became so extensive that in some sectors it even embraced the PCI as a means of compensating the party for its permanence in opposition.

Second, in relation to the political left, Italy developed an anomaly – the absence of a genuine social democratic party – which was the result of a double contradiction: a communist party which continued to define itself as such despite increasingly resembling – at least in several respects – a social-democratic party, and a socialist party that continued to invoke the tradition of social democratic reformism despite failing to conduct a reformist policy of any note after a decade in power (Coen, 1989). This anomaly, moreover, explained the dilemma of the political system as a whole, for as long as it persisted, no alternation in government was possible.

Third, in relation to the PCI, the party, having peaked electorally in 1976, suffered an inexorable decline thereafter in both votes and members. By the 1980s the party was experiencing considerable difficulties, which were exacerbated by the sudden death of its charismatic leader, Enrico Berlinguer, in 1984. Deeply divided over its future strategy, the party appointed a member of the old guard, Alessandro Natta, who was a safe candidate insofar as his appointment did not generate opposition from the two wings of the party (the left led by Pietro Ingrao and the right led by Giorgio Napolitano). Natta was viewed, and viewed himself, as a 'night watchman', a candidate who would give the party more time to find a leader for the long term. While acutely aware of the need to renovate the PCI he also knew that any moves in this direction were likely to ignite conflict between the factions in the party. He consequently shunned innovation, and the PCI's stagnation and decline continued. In the 1987 general election the party's vote dropped to 26.6 per cent, the lowest level since 1963. Further damaging results followed in the local elections of May 1988. Natta – who was unwell, having suffered a heart attack during the local election campaign – took an unprecedented decision for a PCI leader and resigned, indicating in his letter of resignation that the party needed more incisive leadership. He was replaced by Achille Occhetto (Bull, 1989).

Occhetto's rise to power

At the time of his election Occhetto was, at 52, the second youngest leader in the PCI's history (Berlinguer had been 50). He was born in Turin on 3 March 1936. His parents wanted to call him Akel, after the mythical Danish explorer, but the fascist register of births would not accept foreign names so they chose Achille instead (but this explains why the Italian media dubbed him 'Akel' in later years). He was of middle-class, Catholic (he was baptised) background, and subject early on to the influence of intellectual and political debate. His father, a director of one of the largest publishing houses in Italy, Einaudi, had been a follower of the resistance movement and one of the founders of the short-lived political movement 'Christian Left' (sinistra cristiana). The house in Turin was frequented by members of the intellectual left such as Italo Calvino, Natalia Ginzburg and Cesare Pavese, who (Occhetto recalls) used to help him with his Latin homework. For a while he was active in the Catholic interest group, Catholic Action. He was therefore, like many Italians, subject to the combined influence of Catholicism and revolutionary change, and as a consequence the possible nexus between Catholicism and communism always fascinated him. Which of these doctrines influenced him most was never in doubt, and was perhaps best symbolised in his family life: he married three times (to his third wife in 1988), and his two children (by his second wife) were named after the American black leader Malcom X and the Mexican revolutionary Emiliano Zapata. After school he went to university in Milan to read philosophy, and it was at university that he became active in politics.

He was from early on a gifted orator and a strong personality, and was renowned in his youth for doing good imitations mainly of older communists. He quickly established himself as intelligent, quick, gifted, experimental and determined, and at the same time impassioned, emotional and sensitive (the accusation in 1989 that he wanted simply to 'kill off' the PCI deeply upset him). He was also, in the 1960s, one of a new breed of communists who refused to adopt *il look grigio* (the grey look) so typical of his generation. He did not shy from wearing splashes of loud colour and other 'modern' accoutrements such as waistcoats, velvet suits, bow ties, long woollen scarves and half-moon glasses. Yet perhaps his most distinguishing characteristic – particularly when combined with his pipe – was his thick moustache, which he grew whilst on holiday in 1968 and never shaved off. Unlike his thick mop of brushed-back hair, his *baffi* went grey prematurely, the most visible physical sign of that 'grey' tradition from whence he came (D'Agata, 1990, pp. 5–16; Lorusso, 1992, ch. 1).

Occhetto entered the PCI through its youth movement (the FGCI), of which he was leader between 1962 and 1966. He was to the left of the party, supporting not only the positions of the Ingrao left but also the more radical positions of the student movement in the late 1960s. This earned him eight years 'in exile' in Sicily as leader of the provincial section of the party in Palermo. Yet if the coincidence of his period in the youth movement with the rise of radicalism in and beyond the party had given him a rebellious tinge, the period in Sicily and thereafter revealed him to be a real *figlio d'apparato* (party man). He rose to become regional leader of the party in Sicily in 1972, the first time a non-Sicilian had held this position, and became a faithful supporter of Berlinguer's 'Historic Compromise' strategy (launched in 1973), which was based on seeking a governing agreement with the DC rather than an alternative to it.

Elected to the Chamber of Deputies in 1976, Occhetto returned to the party headquarters in Rome the following year to coordinate a working group on the party's medium-term plan and to take responsibility for the schools and universities section of the party.

From there he worked his way up through the party. He entered the secretariat in 1983, becoming responsible for the party's southern section. By that time he had become a member of the central group. He was given formal responsibility for the running of the campaign for the European elections in 1984, during which Berlinguer suddenly died and – largely because of the huge sympathy vote which resulted – the PCI, for the first time in the postwar period, obtained a higher percentage of the vote than the DC (the so-called *sorpasso*). Occhetto's name was circulated alongside Alessandro Natta, Giorgio Napolitano and Luciano Lama as a possible successor to Berlinguer. From his comments it appears that he was quite fearful of being handed the reins of power at that moment and was relieved that Natta was chosen (Lorusso, 1992, pp. 123–4).

Nevertheless, despite this hesitancy he rapidly became Natta's right-hand man, both influencing the leader's thinking and terminology and drawing on the support of a nucleus of *quarantenni* (the younger generation in their forties) who held important posts in the party: Massimo D'Alema, Piero Fassino, Fabio Mussi and Walter Veltroni. The 1987 election defeat caused open protest in the party and demands for drastic changes in the leadership. Natta's offer to resign was rejected at an emergency meeting of the *direzione* (leadership), and the leader then proposed making Occhetto deputy leader (*viceseg-retario*). Natta justified this unprecedented move (strictly not provided for in the party statute, indicating, as it clearly did, an heir apparent) on the grounds of continuity. If this sounded rather odd (considering the apparent failure of the existing leadership), Natta was undoubt-edly making the proposal in the knowledge that other names were being aired by different wings of the party (including that of D'Alema by the right) and that this would secure Occhetto's safe passage when the time came. The proposal, although (to the grassroots) a welcome sign of change, divided the party at the top, Napolitano's *miglioristi* voting against it and a majority in favour being formed by an alliance between the followers of Berlinguer (*berlingueriani*) and those of Ingrao (*ingraiani*).

Occhetto's elevation, then, changed the internal balance of power, ending the centre-right majority which had supported the leadership since the seventeenth Congress in 1986. His almost unanimous elec-tion (there were five abstentions) to the leadership just over a year later (on 21 June 1988) was due largely to the absence of other candi-dates. In short, Occhetto's route to the leadership of the PCI was the result of a curious mixture of, on the one hand, the unorthodox (insofar as he was made heir apparent) and, on the other, the typical communist practice of cooption followed by unanimity around a single candidate.

Occhetto's key role in the PCI-PDS transformation

One of the problems for Occhetto in history's judgement of him is that he made his controversial proposal to dissolve the PCI only five days after the collapse of the Berlin Wall, and the link with the international changes which this event symbolised was made explicit. As a consequence, it has become a popular misconception that Occhetto's decision was little more than an ill-thought-out, knee-jerk reaction to the transformation of the PCI's international environment. Indeed, this was precisely the criticism levelled at him from the left of the party, which opposed his action, while the right of the party regarded it as tardy acceptance of the inevitable. Yet it is important to remember that Occhetto became leader of the PCI a good year before the collapse of the Berlin Wall, and during that year he embarked on the most ambitious programme of reform in the party's history. This is not to underestimate the influence of the collapse of communism on his decision; but rather to underline the extent to which Occhetto's own programme of change in the previous year made such a decision more consistent and explicable than would otherwise have been the case, a programme of change, moreover, which was overshadowed and largely forgotten by what subsequently happened.

As the new leader in 1988, Occhetto's response to the PCI's decline was immediate. He abandoned Natta's policy of cautious renewal and proposed a 'refounding' of the party itself. While not without historical precedent, the infrequency of such a proposal – Antonio Gramsci in 1926 and Palmiro Togliatti in 1944 were the only two other examples – suggested that this would be more than just rhetoric. Indeed, as if to reinforce his conviction, Occhetto borrowed two Togliattian phrases from the 1940s to characterise his proposals: *nuovo partito* (new party) and *nuovo corso* (new course). Altering several of the operational rules of the party congress to ensure that genuine reform could not be prevented by the traditional need for unanimity, Occhetto achieved several critical changes to the distinctive features of the PCI's identity at the eighteenth congress, held in March 1989 (Bull, 1991b). Democratic centralism was completely dismantled, the teleological nature of the party and the concept of a 'third way' was finally ended (with unequivocal acceptance of the market economy and capital accumulation), and the party's Marxist heritage was called into question through the deletion of all references to Togliatti, Labriola, Gramsci and Lenin in the new party statute and all but one reference to Marx ('The free development of each is the free development of all'). The party retained its links to some traditions of the workers' movement but was nonetheless a 'non-ideological organisation'. Moreover, in contrast with party tradition, where change was always couched in the language of continuity, this was explicitly recognised as a break with the past: *discontinuità* (discontinuity).

These changes were achieved without damaging party unity. Moreover Occhetto's authority was enhanced by a generational change in the party leadership (which saw the entry of the so-called 'forty year olds' and the capturing of the key positions by his 'young colonels'), his own election as secretary (by 235 votes to two with six abstentions, the first by secret ballot in the party's history) and a creditable showing for the PCI in the European elections three months later. Had the PCI, then, at its eighteenth congress effectively 'crossed the ford'? For Eugenio Scalfari, the editor of the influential daily *La Repubblica* and a close personal friend of Occhetto, he had not only achieved this (the change of name now apparently being only a formality) but had done so while holding a substantial (28 per cent) percentage of the party's electorate intact, a major achievement (Scalfari, 1989a, 1989b). The congress was generally hailed as a huge personal triumph for Occhetto. Yet had Scalfari been right, the subsequent revolutions in Eastern Europe would not have had the impact they did on the PCI, because the issues they raised would already have been dealt with and buried at the eighteenth congress.

Scalfari's assessment was overly optimistic for three reasons. First, it underestimated the significance of the changes which still needed to be carried through to complete the transition. The PCI had not unequivocally renounced its heritage, Togliatti's name still adorned the front page of the party weekly *Rinascita*, the party's name and symbol (the hammer and sickle) remained intact, as did the party anthems (despite Occhetto's attempt to remove them at the congress). Furthermore the party's international alignment remained unclear because the aspiration (strongly expressed by the right of the party) to become a core component of Western social democracy was clouded by a concomitant desire (expressed by the left of the party) to embrace Gorbachevism, the Catholic world's more radical elements and progressive social movements.

Second, Scalfari's assessment underestimated the extent to which these issues would generate opposition inside the party, particularly from the left, which had different views on how far the party should go in its transition. Moreover, discussion at the eighteenth congress had revealed that it was difficult to renounce certain principles without embracing new ones at the same time, a problem which had yet to be addressed.

Third, one of the changes carried through at the congress had a paradoxical effect insofar as it made completion of the transition more difficult. The complete dismantling of the principle of democratic centralism was essential to ridding the party of a fundamental communist tenet. Yet at the same time it removed the old constraints on free discussion and dissent from the party line, providing dissenters with legitimate means to try to prevent further changes from being carried through. At the same time the first elections by secret ballot of the top organs of the party, the *direzione* and the *segretaria* (both elected by the Central Committee), witnessed a strengthening of those very forces (on the left) which would ultimately oppose the completion of the transition.

This dilemma became quickly apparent once Occhetto embarked on the second phase of the transition after the congress. This phase was

Occhetto: 'We can't chop off our roots!'

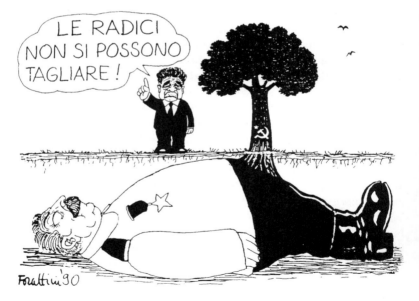

Reproduced with the kind permission of Giorgio Forattini

to be characterised by two initiatives: tackling the remnants of the party's 'distinctiveness' (its national Marxist heritage and international alignment); and imparting changes to the party periphery through action at the level of the party federations. The latter action was due to begin in the autumn but was abandoned due to the turn of events. The former began in the summer but quickly ran into serious difficulties as the forces of the left in the party, drawing on the new resources of legitimised open debate within the party, put up fierce resistance to any further moves towards the social democratisation of the PCI. In the face of this resistance, Occhetto and the leadership hesitated, stalled and even partially retreated (Bull, 1991b, pp. 112–14). The summer of 1989, then, marked an effective halt to the reform programme embarked on a year before and the PCI appeared to be hovering on the verge of a crisis. How Occhetto would have attempted to overcome the opposition to the completion of his reform programme will probably never be clear because the revolutions in Eastern Europe radically changed the parameters of the debate and brought matters to a head.

The speed with which the developments in Eastern Europe occurred make Occhetto's reform programme appear cautious in nature. Having been historically in the vanguard of change in the international communist movement, the PCI now found itself confronted with East European communist parties (beginning with that in Hungary) unequivocally shedding their communist identities and applying for membership of the Socialist International. The party's problematic international alignment was brutally exposed as the issue rapidly began to change from one of giving support to a leader (Gorbachev) committed to reforming socialism to one of responding to the collapse of a socialist bloc and the throwing out of socialism altogether. Similarly, the PCI's reluctance to shed its Marxist heritage began to cast a different light on the party in the new international situation. A party which had appeared to have virtually 'crossed the ford' in March now appeared almost hard line in comparison with its counterparts in Eastern Europe and the pressure intensified on the PCI to follow their example.

Yet the manner in which Occhetto responded shocked the party and the wider political world. The collapse of the Berlin Wall prompted him to bypass the traditional channels of policy making in the party, and five days later he proposed the dissolution of the PCI and the founding of a new non-communist party of the left. Occhetto argued that the revolutions in Central and Eastern Europe had placed a new phase on the agenda in Italian politics, and that the PCI could not could not wait for this phase to begin but had to initiate it. In the fiercest denunciation of 'real socialism' ever made by a leader of the PCI, he said that in the East 'not only did socialism fail, in some countries it was not even tried'. That tradition now needed to be unequivocally left behind. Exulting the PCI's 'originality', he said, was no longer sufficient: the party had to recognise that even the best of its traditions were conceived and inspired within the logic of bloc politics. In the new situation the PCI was no longer an adequate instrument of change, and what was required therefore was a break with the past (Bull, 1991b, pp. 35–6). This proposal threw the PCI into its deepest crisis since its founding. The party failed to unify behind him, and the opposition this time came not just from the pro-Soviets (around Armando Cossutta) and the Ingrao left but also from leading figures in the old guard (including former leader Natta) who had always supported the leadership, thus shattering the internal system of alliances by which the leadership had traditionally ruled.

Consequently, it took fifteen months and two bitterly contested congresses to transform the party. The nineteenth congress, held in March 1990, dissolved the PCI and initiated a 'constituent phase' during which *la cosa* (the thing) – as the 'non-party' was referred to – was meant to be moulded into a new non-communist party in time for its official birth at the PCI's final congress (Bull and Daniels, 1990). This phase was meant to incorporate a considerable number of non-PCI sympathisers too. Yet it became a deeply internal affair, characterised by a struggle between old party factions. Opponents of Occhetto's proposal refused to accept the congress's decision. Arguing that the PCI still existed (because its final congress was scheduled) and asserting the sovereignty of the congress (that is, no congress could bind its successor), they proposed the creation of a 'refounded' communist party at the twentieth congress, and the debate which had apparently exhausted itself in the run-up to the nineteenth congress continued in similar vein. Yet Occhetto's majority was never in doubt, and the key issue at the twentieth congress was less whether or not the new party (The Democratic Party of the left, PDS) would be launched than whether Occhetto could convince the bulk of the opposition (mainly the Ingrao left) to go into the new party rather than breaking away to form an alternative political force. This was achieved through a tactical radicalisation of the party line over the issue of the Gulf War, although in the end Occhetto failed to prevent the breakaway of the more orthodox pro-Soviets, who formed a smaller new party,

Rifondazione comunista ('Communist Refoundation') (Bull, 1991c).

This then, was, no victory celebration. As if to underline it, at about the same time as the PCI and PDS flags were being exchanged at the party HQ, Occhetto was personally humiliated by the last act of the congress when he failed, as the only candidate, to get elected as leader of the new party. Both the right and the left wished to register their unhappiness with the outcome of the congress (the former because of the radicalisation of the party line and the latter because of the dissolution of the PCI) by reducing Occhetto's victory to underwhelming proportions. However, they underestimated how high the number of abstentions would be owing to the fact that delegates had already left the congress, and this, coupled with the new party statute's requirement for the leader to receive an absolute majority of the votes of all the members of the new council rather than a simple majority of those voting, ensured the worst possible start for the PDS and a personal humiliation for Occhetto, who stormed out of the congress saying 'Find yourself another General Secretary'. In a rearranged vote a few days later the party rallied behind him with over 70 per cent support, but the damage was done and an inauspicious start had been made.

Occhetto as leader of the PDS

Occhetto was leader of the PDS from its founding in January 1991 until June 1994, when he resigned. This period was the most politically convulsive in postwar Italian history for it marked the complete collapse of the parties which had ruled Italy for the past fifty years. This was largely (but not only) the consequence of an anticorruption campaign pursued by Italian magistrates, who exposed a massive system of bribery and corruption operated by the DC and PSI in order to reinforce their hold on power. This campaign to root out corruption began in early 1992 and in the short space of two years saw the organisational and electoral collapse of both parties, the arrest of hundreds of their personnel (including former leaders and prime minsters) and the parties' removal from power. The party system, in short, experienced a meltdown in this period in which new political forces quickly surfaced to fill the void left by the old parties (Newell and Bull, 1997).

For Occhetto, this situation represented an unprecedented opportunity. With the meltdown of the party system the PDS was the largest party to remain intact. Moreover Occhetto could claim that its very birth had removed an important linchpin blocking the system – even if it was not solely this which accounted for the changes (Bull and Newell, 1993, pp. 206–15) – by allowing voters freely to abandon Christian democracy when the extent of corruption became clear without the fear of letting in an anti-system communist party. The transition of the PDS, therefore, partly prompted a transition of the party system (and thus the political system) itself. Seen from this perspective, Occhetto's transformation of the PCI into the PDS had not only helped initiate the collapse of the old party system but had also placed the PDS in the best position both to shape the newly emerging political system and to be its first wielder of power.

Yet in April 1994, in the first elections when this opportunity could have been translated into reality, the PDS suffered a crushing electoral defeat at the hands of the alliance which went on to form the most right-wing governing coalition in Italy's postwar history (containing, for the first time since Mussolini, fascist ministers), whose common rhetoric was virulent anticommunism and whose principal political force (Forza Italia) had been in existence a bare three months. A similar defeat at the European elections in June left Occhetto with little option but to resign, his experiment with non-communism apparently in tatters, and with the entire period 1988–94 amounting to a huge personal failure. How was this unprecedented opportunity missed? How did Occhetto fail to reap the benefits of one of the most audacious party transitions in modern Western democracy?

The answer lies in a complex set of long-term factors upon which the PDS's ability to exploit the situation it had (partly) created for itself was dependent (Bull, 1994a). Specifically, to be – and to stay – in the vanguard of the changes engulfing the system and thus inherit the fruits of them (in the form of entering government) the PDS needed to be strong, united, sufficiently 'new' and have a feasible alliance strategy. These qualities proved to be more elusive than expected. First, although still the largest organisation, the party's electoral and organisational strength suffered a steep decline as a result of the transition. The PDS emerged from its first major electoral test (the April 1992 national elections) with a 10.5 per cent drop in the share of the vote enjoyed by the PCI in 1987 (McCarthy, 1993), and the party lost 330 240 members between 1990 and 1991 (a figure three times as high as the 1989–90 loss and eight times as high as the 1988–89 loss). These figures suggest, therefore, not only that the PDS was failing to reverse the PCI's long-term decline but also that it had steepened as a result of the turmoil the party had undergone, the birth of a new communist party (Communist Refoundation) and the alienation of many traditional militants.

Second, the deep divisions generated by the transition were carried over into the new party, partly as a result of Occhetto's success in convincing the Ingrao left to go into the PDS rather than breaking away to form a new party. This, coupled with the fact that 'new blood' had been discouraged from entering the PDS because of the stranglehold exercised over the transformation by PCI-style factionalism, resulted in a party which was deeply divided at birth over its very identity. The dispute between these factions was not only analogous to what had become a stale debate in the old PCI, but was also more debilitating because of the greater degree of democracy inside the new party, where factions could form freely and attempt to undermine the outcome of the transformation. Symptomatic of this was the Ingrao left's decision to form a faction called the 'Democratic Communists', something which indicated the direction in which they would take the new party if they obtained control of the leadership.

The disunity of the party and its parallels with the old PCI undermined its claims to 'newness' and that it represented a distinct break with the past. It was further undermined by the anticorruption campaign, which began to make inroads into the higher echelons of the PDS ranks. The PCI's share in the DC's 'spoils system' had led to corrupt practices in some sectors of the party, and the PDS, as the organisational heir to the PCI and housing most of its personnel, had to bear the brunt of the exposure of corruption in the party ranks in the early 1990s. By the summer of 1993 over 70 members of the party were officially under investigation for corruption, and many of them had been arrested. This number increased considerably after October 1993, when the former leader of the PSI, Bettino Craxi, began cooperating with the magistrates and exposing a number of apparently illicit PCI activities. The allegations – including illegal funding from the Soviet Union, participation in a KGB-run network in Italy and sharing in many of the kickbacks in contracts for transport, construction and large industry – became progressively more serious both in import and in the personnel involved. In January 1994 (only three months before the national elections) Massimo D'Alema (Occhetto's second in command) was officially placed under investigation for illicit funding activities, and rumours abounded that Occhetto himself was next on the list.

The corruption issue threatened to engulf the PDS and threw Occhetto into a paradoxical dilemma. To defend the PDS he emphasised the difference between the individual or isolated instances of PCI/PDS corruption and the *system* of corruption operated by the DC and PSI. The PDS, he emphasised, had a 'clean face'; the party had always been and remained 'different' from all the others, and many of the accusations, it was suggested, constituted a plot to prevent the left from coming to power. This position became increasingly unconvincing and difficult to sustain as the allegations and arrests climbed the party hierarchy. More importantly, the generic argument of 'distinctiveness' (*diversità*) represented a backwards step with regard to the new party's objective, which was to free the PDS from this type of association. This prompted ferocious internal debate and retarded the development of a new culture inside the party, unwittingly giving support to those inside the PDS who had opposed the PCI's transformation (Bull, 1994b). In the run-up to the elections, therefore, Occhetto found himself making inconsistent statements. On the one hand, in response to the criticism that the party was still 'communist', he argued that it was no longer 'different' from other parties; on the other hand, in response to accusations of corruption in the party ranks, he argued the reverse. Moreover there was a sense in which he was losing both arguments, with the PDS being perceived as still 'communist' but no 'different' from the other parties when it came to the so-called 'moral issue'. The situation was testing even the most loyal militants and voters.

Finally, to inherit the fruits of the Italian transition the PDS needed an effective alliance strategy. This was not only because the party was not big enough to gain power by itself, but also because the electoral system was reformed during 1993–94, introducing a (primarily) majoritarian system which placed pressure on all parties to seek out allies in order to ensure representation in the new parliament and gain from Italy's transition towards a bipolarised party system of two broad and competing alliances (to the left and to the right). Occhetto again found himself in a curious dilemma. It had always been assumed that the ending of the 'communist question' would open up the prospect of a united left specifically through an alliance between the PSI and the organisational heir of the PCI, thus overcoming the historic communist–socialist split of 1921. Yet what had not been expected was that the transformation of the PCI would be accompanied by the electoral and organisational collapse of the PSI. The PDS therefore had effectively to rebuild the left (or the centre-left) from the myriad of new groups and parties which had mushroomed after the collapse of the old party system. The result was an unwieldy centre-left coalition (the Progressive Alliance) of no less than eight small (except for the PDS) parties stretching from the progressive centre to the extreme left (including Communist Refoundation). Such was the diversity of interests contained within it that the alliance lacked a clear programme and failed to unite behind a single leader. It did not look credible, therefore, as a governing alliance, and it was outwitted in the competition with the right-wing alliance led by Silvio Berlusconi, who exploited the presence of communists in the alliance by mounting a ferocious assault on the PDS and the progressives as old-style *statalisti* (state-lovers) (Bull, 1996, pp. 168–9).

There are, of course, more detailed psephological explanations for the PDS's electoral defeat in 1994 (Bull and Newell, 1995). The general argument being made here, however, is that in the period 1989–94 the PDS, far from being a 'new' party guiding Italy's transition in such a way as to be the chief beneficiary, resembled more a party on the edge of a vortex (one which had already claimed the DC and the PSI) and trying to ensure its own survival. Italy's transition, then, undermined the success of the very transformation (from PCI to PDS) which had partially prompted it. As a consequence, while Occhetto could claim that his first two objectives had been achieved (the transformation of the PCI and of the party system), the third (the victory of the left and entry into government) had not only eluded him but had done so despite what had been widely perceived as the greatest opportunity for the left to gain power since the war. The unexpected scale of the defeat to a nascent political force allied with neofascists left Occhetto with little option but to resign as leader: 'when he announced his resignation, the failure of anyone in the party leadership to issue the obligatory call for him to reconsider his decision bespoke the depths of his disgrace' (Kertzer, 1996, p. 170).

An assessment of Occhetto's role

There are two questions which should be considered to assess Occhetto's role in the PCI–PDS transformation and his leadership of the PDS. First, what was the exact motivation behind Occhetto's decision to dissolve the PCI in the autumn of 1989 and how much of a difference did it make that Occhetto was leader of the party at the time rather than someone else (for example, Natta)? Second, was the failure of the PDS to gain power in 1994 a personal failure (Occhetto's) or was it largely beyond the leader's control?

The first question is difficult to answer definitively, because neither

Occhetto's public speeches nor extensive interviews with Occhetto himself (see Occhetto, 1994) provide a clear idea of what was going on in his head. For many it was the suddenness of the decision which makes it difficult to explain in any rational or systematic way, something commented on most forcefully by Neil Kinnock, who had met Occhetto on the Friday before the latter's dramatic announcement:

> I asked Occhetto if the PCI could change its name and he replied to me, pronouncing carefully three times, 'It is very difficult, very difficult, very difficult'. Having returned to London, I saw, in huge letters, in Monday's newspaper, *The PCI changes name*. If he had said to me 'it's difficult' only once, he would have already changed [the name] by Saturday (quoted in Occhetto, 1994, p. 64).

Yet it would be a mistake to assume that the speed with which he reached his decision meant that it was either ill-thought out or reflected a sudden change of mind. It is clear, in fact, that the issue had long been taxing him. According to Occhetto himself, 'In reality, for me it had become a real obsession. And every meeting, every conversation constituted an opportunity to gauge reactions to the possibility of changing the name [of the party]. But they were indirect soundings, never on the basis of a complete proposal' (ibid., pp. 64–5). The validity of these comments is reinforced by the historical record, and specifically Occhetto's reform programme launched a year before. True, the outcome of that programme was never made clear (and it is likely that even Occhetto himself was unaware of what might transpire) but it did not exclude a possible transformation of the party; on the contrary, as suggested above, it can be seen as an attempt to achieve a transformation (that is, social democratisation) of the party on a *gradual* basis. A more accurate question, therefore, might be less 'what motivated Occhetto to dissolve the party?' than 'what motivated Occhetto to move from a gradual to a rapid strategy of transformation?' To answer this question one has to consider the options open to Occhetto in November 1989.

Theoretically there were two options. The first was to continue with his reform programme as originally envisaged. The second was to take more drastic action, enacting change by short-cutting the traditional party channels. The only real argument in favour of the former option was the possible consequences of following the latter option. While short-cutting the traditional channels was not unprecedented (the former leader, Berlinguer, had done so in launching the 'Historic

Compromise' for example), resorting to such methods ran the risk of severely dividing the party. Having already seen the degree of opposition sparked off in the summer over the party's heritage and international alignment, Occhetto was aware that a radical proposal made without first consulting the leading party organs would plunge the PCI into a deep internal crisis. The arguments against this position, however, made continuing with the original reform programme an unrealistic option in practice: Occhetto's hand was effectively forced by two factors.

The first was the increasing isolation in which the party found itself at the national and international levels. At the national level the PCI's standing with the media, the other parties and (potentially) the electorate rapidly changed for the worst. From a position of receiving support and encouragement for his reform programme, Occhetto now found himself derided for his lack of progressiveness compared with the leadership of the parties in Eastern and Central Europe. The speed with which the changes continued in Eastern and Central Europe made the PCI's reasons for its inaction (that Italian communism stood for something different and that programmes were more important than names) appear ever less convincing. At the international level, in the new situation, the Socialist International (SI) quickly began to assume considerable importance, declaring itself the forum for socialist parties of the East and West. The organisation looked set to become the international home for the newly emerging parties in Central and Eastern Europe. For the PCI, which had always claimed an important role in the liberalisation of Central and Eastern Europe, marginalisation beckoned as parties such as the Hungarian socialist party submitted applications to joint the SI, while Italy continued to be represented by the PSI.

The second factor related to the internal state of the PCI. By early autumn Occhetto's initial fear of dividing the party by making a sudden announcement began to lose relevance as internal divisions intensified to a critical stage under the pressure of international events and in the absence of the demands of democratic centralism. It was hardly the case, then, that Occhetto, in making his announcement, would have divided an erstwhile united party. The PCI was deep in crisis and visibly fragmenting.

What the above argument suggests is that while, theoretically speaking, the options by the autumn of 1989 appeared to be between continuing the reform programme or taking a leap forward, in reality the options were between sliding backwards or taking a leap forward.

In the previous year Occhetto had taken the party towards a precipice of change. His intention had been to master the climb down with sufficient safety ropes to hold the party and its electorate together. The situation which had arisen by the autumn of 1989 meant that this option was no longer open to him. Carrying through profound changes was a long and arduous business. The party's entire history was witness to this, as was Occhetto's existing reform programme. Continuing with it at that stage meant effectively sliding backwards because the international situation had overtaken it. The choice, then, was between sliding back from the precipice or leaping into it and hoping that the speed of change, coupled with the argument that this was simply an acceleration of his existing reform programme (and therefore a form of continuity and not a radical break) would persuade the party to rally behind him. Occhetto, in short, was happy to 'jump' when 'pushed'.

Moreover, once the announcement was made a momentum was created which inspired Occhetto to carry it through. Occhetto has commented that although he was, in his initial announcement, only airing a proposal, by the next day the media were presenting it as a decision already taken (particularly in view of the unconventional way in which it was made); and because Occhetto then realised that this confusion would generate hostility and opposition within the party ranks, he brought forward his plans and stayed up all night to type (on a typewriter, the two-fingered way) a complete proposal, handing the pages to his wife to read as he wrote them, ready to present to the *Segretaria* the next morning: 'When Aureliana understood the direction in which I was heading, she did not want to continue, worried about what I was going to confront' (Occhetto, 1994, p. 65).

The fact that the party failed to rally behind him (or at least to the extent he had hoped) and the fact that those who opposed him included key figures in the old guard, including his predecessor Natta, suggests that had Occhetto not been leader, then history would have been different. The idiosyncratic way in which he chose to launch his proposal reinforces this view: it was a personal decision and he was willing to bear the consequences. It could be argued, then, that had Natta remained as leader he would not have proposed the dissolution of the PCI and it is a matter of conjecture as to what might have subsequently happened. True as this may be, however, it is important to emphasise the precise point at which Occhetto's leadership made a difference, for, as the above analysis suggests, it would be a simplification to argue that Occhetto changed the tide of history by the proposal he made in November 1989. Had Natta remained leader then the crucial changes to the PCI's identity – which in 1988–89, brought the PCI to the brink of change and effectively removed Occhetto's options in November 1989 – would never have occurred. Consequently it could be argued that, while Occhetto's leadership did make a difference, it was his decision in 1988 to embark on a fundamental programme of gradual reform which shaped subsequent events. This momentous decision was taken before the collapse of communism in Central and Eastern Europe and in the absence of any knowledge that it was likely to happen, which is testimony to the originality and significance of the idea.

The second question (how inevitable was the failure of his leadership?) assumes that Occhetto's leadership during the transition *was* a failure (or at least a failure *tout court*), and this can only be properly answered through an understanding of the post-Occhetto period: his legacy.

Occhetto's legacy

Within two years of Occhetto's humiliating electoral defeat the new leader of the party, Massimo D'Alema (who had been opposed by Occhetto in favour of Walter Veltroni), had reformulated the PDS's electoral alliance and secured a stunning victory at the 1996 elections, whereupon the party, for the first time in its history, entered the government as part of the 'Olive Tree Coalition' (*Ulivo*). This tends to suggest that Occhetto's failure was fundamentally an electoral one, and that D'Alema managed to overcome this by making the PDS more electorally attractive. Yet it would be reductionist to argue that Occhetto's failure amounted to an electoral defeat, if for no other reason than the fact that the turnaround in electoral fortunes between 1994 and 1996 was due to several factors which went beyond any individual leader's personal abilities (Newell and Bull, 1996). D'Alema's greater success was not due to any radical renovation of the PDS itself; rather the myriad of left and centre parties were able to learn from their mistakes in 1994, and this time successfully forged an electoral alliance which was able to defeat a disunited and weaker right. Indeed the victory of the *Ulivo* was more the product of the changes in the make-up of the principal alliances on both left and right than of a significant realignment of the electorate in support of the PDS.

To locate the exact nature of Occhetto's failure (and thus evaluate the extent of his achievement) it is necessary to focus specifically on the PDS and the shape of the political left in general, for it can be argued that the election victory of 1996 did not resolve the essential dilemma which Occhetto had bequeathed the left by enacting the transition of the PDS and thereby contributing to the transition of the political system itself. It was clear at the time of Occhetto's resignation in 1994 that the PDS, paradoxically, constituted a source of both strength and weakness on the left in the changed party political system. On the one hand, with the collapse of the PSI the PDS was the only substantial organisation on the left, having approximately 700 000 members and commanding something like 80 per cent of all left-of-centre electoral support. It therefore had to be the linchpin of any future electoral victory. At the same time, however, this organisational and electoral strength prompted considerable division on the left, undermining any moves towards either a permanent alliance or a single party, because the smaller parties feared being absorbed by a party which, for them, still had evident continuities with an organisation (the PCI) whose very essence was anathema to almost all of them.

It is in this respect that in 1994, Occhetto's transformation was regarded by many, as a failure. The transformation of the PCI into the PDS was meant to result in a new single party of the left, which, in overcoming Italy's anomaly (the absence of a social-democratic party) would attract disillusioned socialist voters, progressive Catholics, the so-called 'lost left' (disillusioned with both socialism and communism) and newly-enfranchised voters at the same time as holding on to erstwhile communist supporters. It failed to do this, largely because, despite a radical break with the past, Occhetto could not prevent the internal dynamics of the transformation and the new party from being captured by old party *apparatchiks*, such were the divisions generated by his original proposal. The identity of the PDS ultimately remained unclear, and its ambivalence was perhaps best symbolised by the maintenance of the old PCI symbol, the hammer and sickle, at the base of the oak tree symbol of the PDS. It was becoming increasingly accepted by 1994 (although not openly spoken about within the party itself) that the PDS did not have the potential to attract such a wide range of voters. Indeed, the failure of the PCI–PDS transformation, coupled with the other changes in Italian politics to which it had contributed, had simply exacerbated the fragmentation of the left, multiplying the number of small parties instead of concentrating them into a single organisation. Hence, what was on the agenda, although Occhetto and the PDS refused to countenance it, was the dissolution of the PDS and the building of a new party from scratch.

What reinforces this argument is that the 1996 election victory did not resolve this dilemma. If anything, it helped ignite the debate in the party, since the *Ulivo* demonstrated at least the electoral potential of a centre-left party if one could be built. Consequently, D'Alema began, while the party was actually in government, a second transformation of the PDS, one which resulted in its dissolution in January 1997 at its second congress, the creation of *Cosa 2* ('the second thing'), which was open to all components of the left, and its conversion into the Democrats of the Left one year later (Bull, 1997). This party was designed to unite the left and thus overcome Italy's long-standing anomaly. Whether it will do so is too early to tell, but this development puts Occhetto's failure – and therefore his achievements – in clearer perspective.

In staking his place in history, Occhetto claims to be the architect not only of the *svolta* (historical turning point) in the PCI but also of the broader political system itself. According to Occhetto, had he only been the architect of the former, then the issue of the transformation of the PCI would have been more straightforward in that it would have been largely an internal communist affair (Occhetto, 1994, pp. 72–3). Even if some would argue that Occhetto's claim is exaggerated, there can be little doubt that his unexpected announcement in the autumn of 1989 hastened the collapse of the old Italian political order. Yet the extent of the collapse surprised even Occhetto, and it was precisely this combination of change (party *and* regime) which paradoxically proved to be Occhetto's undoing, for it is probably fair to say that the PDS was born to navigate waters in which Occhetto knew all the tides, buoys and sandbanks. Yet the PDS, once born, quickly found itself in a political situation which was undergoing a real sea change, the outcome of which was far from clear. The extent of this change meant that, like the PCI before it, the PDS was not radical or innovative enough to exploit fully the Italian transition (even though its birth was radical and innovatory in and of itself). The birth of the PDS, while helping to unleash broader political changes, became a victim of those changes, and if the political left was to progress it had to be superseded. The party was an agent of change, but found itself spanning both old and new, unable to unite the left and hence on the verge of being left behind.

This is why, ultimately, Occhetto had to go, because it is doubtful that, had he remained leader, he would have taken the decision, as D'Alema subsequently did, to dissolve the PDS in order to further the cause of a single party of the left. Occhetto was a great transformer, the most innovative communist leader since Togliatti. Yet because the PDS was his baby he failed to see that the PDS was simply a short phase in the transformation of the PCI and the transition of the political system itself. In that respect he might be accused of revealing that innate communist conservatism so evident in Natta before him, and to a certain extent his demise was therefore inevitable: he remained a communist, and therefore his inspirational decision to dissolve the PCI hastened his own demise. Yet it should not be forgotten that the significance of D'Alema's decision to transform the PDS does not rank alongside those of Occhetto in 1988 and 1989. D'Alema could not have made his decision in the absence of Occhetto's truly historical break with a seventy-year tradition. Occhetto made his decisions not only in the context of Natta's failure to do so but also in the face of hostile resistance from a substantial number in his party. Moreover his initial decision in 1988 to embark on a radical reform programme proved to be remarkably prescient with regard to international events. 'Akel' lived up to the name the fascists had refused him: like all great explorers he had the courage to think the unthinkable, and it is in this context that history should judge him.

Achille Occhetto: chronology

1936, 3 March	Born in Turin.
1947	With his sister, Paola, received communion and was baptised.
1953	While at school in Milan, joined the Italian Communist Youth Federation (FGCI).
1956	Strongly condemned the Soviet intervention in Hungary (against the PCI line).
1962	Became leader of the FGCI. Attached himself to the Ingrao left in the PCI.
1966	Leader of the provincial section of the PCI in Palermo, Sicily.
1972	Regional leader of the PCI in Sicily.
1976	Elected to the Chamber of Deputies. Returned to party headquarters in Rome as coordinator of the PCI's medium-term plan and the section responsible for education.
1983	Entered party secretariat, responsible for the southern section.
1984	Director of election campaign for the European elections in June, during which leader Berlinguer unexpectedly died and

	the PCI achieved, for the first time, a higher vote than the Christian Democrats (DC). Quickly established himself as right-hand man of new leader, Alessandro Natta.
1987	Became deputy leader of the PCI and therefore heir apparent to Natta.
1988, April	Natta suffered a heart attack during local election campaign and resigned after election defeat.
1988, 21 June	At 52, became leader of the PCI.
1988 Autumn	Embarked on radical reform of the PCI ('new course' and 'new party').
1989, March	Major internal reforms achieved at the PCI's eighteenth congress.
1989, Summer	Completion of reform programme ran into strong internal opposition.
1989, November	After the collapse of the Berlin Wall, proposed the dissolution of the PCI and the formation of a new non-communist party of the left.
1990, March	PCI's nineteenth congress formally dissolved the PCI and initiated a 'constituent phase' to build a new party, during which the PCI was dubbed 'the thing'.
1991, January	PCI's twentieth (and final) congress confirmed the dissolution of the PCI and gave birth to Democratic Party of the Left (PDS). Occhetto became the first leader of the new party. Pro-Soviets split and formed a smaller new party, 'Communist Refoundation' (RC).
1992, April	In the PDS's first test in the national election the party lost 10.5 per cent of the vote in relation to the old PCI in 1987. Party remained in opposition.
1992–94	Electoral and organisational collapse of the ruling parties (DC and Socialists, PSI), under anticorruption drive of the Italian magistrates, which threatened the PDS too.
1994, January	Formation of the Progressive Alliance for the 1994 elections, consisting of eight parties, including the PDS and the RC.
1994, April	Defeat of the Progressive Alliance in the national elections to a right-wing alliance of the Northern League, the former neofascist party and Forza Italia.
1994 June	Poor electoral showing by the PDS in the European elections. Occhetto resigned as leader. In subsequent contest between Walter Veltroni and Massimo D'Alema for the leadership, weight thrown behind the former who lost. Occhetto became marginalised in the party.
1996, April	After election victory, the PDS came to power as part of the Olive Tree Coalition.
1997, January	The PDS's second congress decided to dissolve the party and build a new party of left. PDS dubbed 'the second thing.'
1998, February	Birth of the 'Democrats of the Left'.

References

Bull, Martin J. (1989) '*Perestroika* is Catching: the Italian Communist Party Elects a New Leader', *Journal of Communist Studies*, vol. 5, no. 1, (March), pp. 79–83.

Bull, Martin J. (1991a) 'Whatever Happened to Italian Communism? Explaining the Dissolution of the Largest Communist Party in the West', *West European Politics*, vol. 14, no. 4 (October).

Bull, Martin J. (1991b) 'The Unremarkable Death of the Italian Communist Party', in Filippo Sabetti and Raimondo Catanzaro (eds), *Italian Politics. A Review. Volume 5* (London: Pinter), pp. 23–39.

Bull, Martin J. (1991c) 'The Italian Communist Party's Twentieth Congress and the Painful Birth of the *Partito Democratico della Sinistra*', *Journal of Communist Studies*, vol. 7, no. 2 (June).

Bull, Martin J. (1994a) 'Another Revolution *Manqué*? The PDS in Italy's Transition 1989–1994', *EUI Working Paper,* SPS No. 94/16 (Florence: European University, Institute).

Bull, Martin J. (1994b) 'Social Democracy's Newest Recruit? Conflict and Cohesion in the Italian Democratic Party of the Left', in David S. Bell and Eric Shaw (eds), *Conflict and Cohesion in Western European Social Democratic Parties* (London: Pinter).

Bull, Martin J. (1996) 'The Great Failure? The Democratic Party of the Left in Italy's Transition', in Stephen Gundle and Simon Parker (eds), *The New Italian Republic: From the Fall of the Berlin Wall to Berlusconi* (London: Routledge).

Bull, Martin J. (1997), 'From PDS to *Cosa 2*. The Second Congress of the Democratic Party of the Left', *EUI Working Paper*, SPS no. 97/3 (Florence: European University Institute).

Bull, Martin J. and Philip Daniels (1990) 'The "New Beginning": the Italian Communist Party under Achille Occhetto', *Journal of Communist Studies*, vol. 6, no. 3 (September).

Bull, Martin J. and James L. Newell (1993) 'Italian Politics and the 1992 Elections: From "Stable Instability" to Instability and Change', *Parliamentary Affairs*, vol. 46, no. 2.

Bull, Martin J. and James L. Newell (1995) 'Italy Changes Course? The 1994 Elections and the Victory of the Right', *Parliamentary Affairs*, vol. 48, no. 1 (January).

Coen, F. (1989) 'La guerra di movimento del generale Occhetto', *La Repubblica*, 28 March.

D'Agata, Salvatore (1990) *Achille Occhetto dalla falce alla quercia* (Rome: Editalia-Edizioni).

Ginsborg, Paul (1990) *A History of Contemporary Italy. Society and Politics 1943–1988* (London: Penguin).

Kertzer, David (1996) *Politics and Symbols. The Italian Communist Party and the Fall of Communism* (New Haven, CT: Yale University Press).

Lorusso, Mino (1992) *Occhetto. Il comunismo italiano da Togliatti al PDS* (Florence: Ponte alle Grazie).

McCarthy, Patrick (1993) 'The Italian Communists Divide – and Do Not Conquer', in Gianfranco Pasquino and Patrick McCarthy (eds), *The End of*

Post-War Politics in Italy. The Landmark 1992 Elections (Boulder, CO: Westview Press).

Newell, James L. and Martin J. Bull (1996) 'The April 1996 Italian General Election: The Left on Top or on Tap?', *Parliamentary Affairs*, vol. 49, no. 4, (October).

Newell, James L. and Martin J. Bull (1997) 'Party Organisations and Alliances in Italy in the 1990s: A Revolution of Sorts', in Martin Bull and Martin Rhodes (eds), 'Crisis and Transition in Italian Politics', special issue of *West European Politics*, vol. 20, no. 1 (January).

Occhetto, Achille (1994) *Il sentimento e la ragione. Un'intervista di Teresa Bartoli* (Milan: Rizzoli).

Pasquino, Gianfranco (1980) *Crisi dei partiti e governabilità* (Bologna: Mulino).

Scalfari, Eugenio (1989a) 'E dopo quarant'anni quella nave approdò...', *La Repubblica*, 18 March.

Scalfari, Eugenio (1989b) 'Il cammello è passato nella cruna dell'ago', *La Repubblica*, 20 June.

General Wojciech Jaruzelski

Martial Law opened the way for dialogue and understanding
(Wojciech Jaruzelski, 1996, p. 454)

General Jaruzelski (*left*) and Lech Walesa sit uneasily together in the Polish Parliament. (*Copyright © Szawomir Sierzputowski, Agencja Gazeta*)

4

General Wojciech Jaruzelski: Hardline Patriot

John Fitzmaurice

> *Martial Law opened the way for dialogue and understanding*
> (Wojciech Jaruzelski, 1996, p. 454)

Two images encapsulate General Jaruzelski. The first is the dramatic and sombre image of the man, in full military uniform, as he broadcast to the Polish people at 6 am on 13 December 1981, announcing that he had declared martial law. The second, in 1989, is of the same general, side by side with Lech Walesa, in the Polish Sejm after the first near-democratic election in Central Europe for forty years. Jaruzelski was the architect of both events; occupier of his own country and liberator. How could this be?

General Jaruzelski remains an enigmatic and mysterious figure, sphinx-like behind the dark glasses he always wears and which were made necessary by the snow-blindness he suffered as a soldier during the Second World War. A communist general of Catholic and aristocratic origins, he was considered a loyal hardliner and a safe pair of hands. He was promoted through the ranks to become Poland's youngest general in 1956. In 1968 he was appointed Polish minister of defence, a sensitive post. Although he always doggedly denied moral responsibility for ordering troops to fire on anticommunist demonstrators in Gdansk in 1970, he could not escape all blame for that bloody incident. In 1981 he declared martial law and outlawed Solidarnosc, putting an end to a unique period of hope in communist Europe. Yet he also presided over the demise of communist control in Poland in 1989/90, and even before that some argue that in 1981 he acted out of patriotic motives: to prevent the economic collapse of Poland and almost certain intervention by the Red Army and possibly other Warsaw Pact armies, as had occurred in Budapest in 1956 and Prague in 1968.

In recent years many Russian and Western historians have been inclined to argue that Soviet intervention was actually not that likely in 1981. But who could really know? The Soviet track record of 1953, 1956, 1968 and 1979 (Afghanistan) was there. Brezhnev, the intervener (albeit reluctantly in 1968), was still in power. As in 1956 and 1968, there had been military manoeuvres. Again, with strong echoes of the events of 1968, there was a crescendo of criticism of Solidarnosc and of the weakness of the PZPR[1] leadership in both the Soviet and GDR press. And as with the ruling Communist Party in Prague in 1968, the PZPR seemed to be losing control. The 1981 Solidarnosc congress had romantically and ill-advisedly demanded free elections and Poland's departure from the Warsaw Pact, both of which had been sticking points for Moscow in 1956 and 1968. The threat was therefore real enough to be taken seriously. It seemed that either the Poles themselves would have to take radical action, or the menace of external intervention would become increasingly likely. From this perspective, a positive view of Jaruzelski's actions would be that he sought, as far as political realities allowed, to permit an independent Polish policy.

But Jaruzelski's policy raises many different questions. Was he a leader of transition by design or default? What were his intentions? What sort of transition did he have in mind? Was he trying to save the party in spite of itself? Was he actually willing to sideline the party to create a new, hybrid regime in the 1981–88 period, based on the triangle of the army/bureaucracy, the Church and a purged civil society? Was he trying to manage transition towards a limited, controlled pluralism based on permanent power-sharing formulas ensuring a permanent though reduced role for the PZPR? Did he intend to eliminate both the old PZPR monopoly and the old Solidarnosc, with their symbiotic relationship? Were his calculations personal, ideological, geopolitical or patriotic?

Who was Wojciech Jaruzelski?

Wojciech Jaruzelski was brought up in a strongly Catholic household. His grandparents were active in Catholic organisations and the whole family went to church on Sundays (Jaruzelski, 1996, p. 98). He attended a Catholic Jesuit gymnasium (grammar school) in Warsaw for six years (1933–39). As he described it, he grew away from religion once he was separated from its institutional structures in the Soviet Union. But he always retained respect for people with faith and never himself gave way to 'vulgar and militant atheism'. He later sought to work with the Church and because of his views felt able to do so on a basis of mutual respect. In 1996 he wrote that he had always had 'a deep respect for the historical values that the Church and religion have brought our people' (ibid., p. 100).

Perhaps the central characteristic of the man was his quality as a soldier. He became a soldier at the age of eighteen, soon after he was deported to Russia. He joined General Zygmunt Bering's army, a deliberate creation of Stalin which stayed in the USSR, took part in the liberation of Poland and became the nucleus of the new army of communist Poland. That he joined Bering's army, which was ultimately to serve the communist cause, rather than General Wladyslaw Anders' army, which was also raised in the USSR but left for the West, seems to have been more a matter of chance circumstance than any deeper choice, as was indeed probably the case for many others.

His bearing, his discipline and preference for order, his distant and slightly mysterious appearance, all can be traced back to his image of himself as first and foremost a soldier, and not a politician, who had risen up through the ranks in time-honoured fashion to become a general. He was reluctant to become prime minister in 1981, telling the Sejm (parliament) that 'As I assume the office of Prime Minister, I would like to assure the House that, as ever, I consider myself first and foremost to be a soldier' (ibid., p. 25).

As a soldier, service to country, duty, discipline and order were his principal virtues and concerns. He clearly tried to bring these same qualities to his work as Prime Minister. Perhaps he accepted the office precisely because he felt that these virtues were lacking in government, that they were needed and that he could introduce them. As Jaruzelski himself ruefully admitted, politics is, in comparison with military command, a quite different and altogether more complex world. Yet in his evaluation of the situation he inherited there was always a political and pragmatic, rather than soldierly and dogmatic, view struggling to get out. It was this pragmatism which enabled him to reach the conclusion that 'we could *come to an understanding with Solidarnosc*' (Ibid., emphasis in original). A pure soldier or a pure ideologue would no doubt have taken a very different stance. This was just one aspect of the enigma of Wojciech Jaruzelski.

A strong sense of Polishness, inflexible patriotism and a tendency to think in historical categories were also central characteristics of the man. His paternal grandfather took part in the 1863 rising against Tsarist Russia and was deported to Siberia for eight years. His father was a volunteer in the 1920 war against Bolshevik Russia. It was therefore 'axiomatic for my generation to maintain and safeguard the re-won and recreated independent Polish State' (ibid., p. 303). He and his family were a living, integral part of the tragic tapestry of Polish history and this historical dimension deeply influenced him. In his youth he had absorbed the traditional Polish anti-Russian and anti-communist attitudes; 'I was brought up in an atmosphere of dislike and, worse, enmity towards Russians. My home, school and the literature I read all taught me an anti-Russian and anti-Soviet attitude' (ibid.)

His ability to think in longer historical terms led him to transcend what he came to see as destructive, suicidal and ultimately irrational attitudes towards Poland's powerful eastern neighbour. His very immersion in Poland's tragic history led him to this ultimately pragmatic conclusion. It was also his historical understanding that all Polish leaders, whatever their own preferences, had been subject to geopolitical limitations on their freedom of action. It was this that led him to adopt a gradualist and 'realistic' attitude towards relations with the Soviet Union, rather than experiencing any sudden conversion on an ideological road to Damascus. At the same time his own situation and experience enabled him to reconcile what appeared to many as unpatriotic, anti-Polish policies, with his strong patriotism.

These strands in Jaruzelski's character, background and experience all came together in his decision to impose martial law in 1981. He wanted, above all, a *Polish* solution and a *moderate* solution that closed no doors for the future. He was prepared, as a soldier on active duty, to take on himself what others were not ready to do, seeing it as a distasteful but necessary duty. He returned to this theme on leaving office as president in 1990, when he assumed complete responsibility for everything that had been done, insisting that nobody else should be held responsible.

These inherent contradictions – semi-aristocratic, Catholic nationalist origins, an early commitment to the communist cause in Poland and a vicar of Bray-like devotion to the Soviet line, but at the same time a flexible, pragmatic and at times apparently contradictory approach – made him what he was: mysterious, enigmatic and hard to read. It allowed everyone – the party hardliners and reformers, the Church hierarchy, the army, the bureaucracy, Moscow and even some of the Solidarnosc opposition – to regard him as a possible partner and ally who could be used. But who used whom? What was Jaruzelski's end game? Did he indeed have one?

Jaruzelski's strategy, 1981 and 1989

In trying to understand the enigma of Wojciech Jaruzelski it is important to seek to reconcile his actions in 1981 and 1988/9. Was there consistency, and if so, what was the thread running through them?

As we have seen, Jaruzelski was a communist and a patriotic Pole, but one who was only too aware of the importance of Poland's giant neighbour. His characteristically pragmatic approach was therefore to be true to what he thought to be the Soviet line at each stage, but interpreted in a Polish way. Thus one discernible thread running through his actions – destroying Home Army remnants in 1947, supporting hardline action in 1970, suppressing Solidarnosc in 1981, turning to it in 1988 – would seem to have been a preference for stability and order but, above all, *Polish* order. In his memoirs he argues that in both 1981 and 1989 he saw himself as being against the wall and as having no other choice but to act in the way he did. Moreover, he claims, the imposition of martial law in 1981 had bought time for a Polish solution, in the sense that he could probably count on being left to himself for as long as Poland seemed under control. In that sense, whilst martial law did not in itself solve anything, it may in the longer term have been, as Jaruzelski himself argues, an important political and psychological precondition of the 1988 opening. It both reassured and caused concern. It reassured Moscow and PZPR bureaucrats and hardliners that Solidarnosc could and would be controlled. It caused concern for Solidarnosc because it demonstrated that what had happened once could happen again. It could be argued that in 1988, as in 1981, Jaruzelski similarly came to recognise a state of necessity, though a very different one. The opening of talks with the old Solidarnosc leaders was obviously a choice of the last resort, not the first resort, but as will be argued below, all other available options had been considered or tried and had not been effective.[2]

It is important, though, to be aware of the dangers of 20/20 hindsight – a cautionary point equally relevant to Jaruzelski's own post-1989 explanations of his actions. The key question is, what did the principal actors know and think at that time? What were the limits of their horizons then? A transitional leader such as Jaruzelski needed to be flexible and pragmatic and probably not too imaginative. After all, in 1988 no one was completely aware of the deep resentment that had been building up against the system, nor could anyone fully imagine the consequences of the ending of the fear of external intervention. 1988 was not 1981, let alone 1956, and new parameters were constantly being set (these even included the possibility of dismantling the system, although no one realised that quite yet). Paradoxically, had the communist decision makers, including Jaruzelski, realised their true weakness, they might have refused to embark on the process, preferring to defend the *status quo* with the still not inconsiderable force that remained at their disposal.

Jaruzelski's 1989 options

What were Jaruzelski's options in 1988/89?[3] It is important to understand that Poland's economic problems formed the backdrop to all that occurred in the 1980–1990 period.

The economy had faced serious problems for several decades, and these were getting worse. Unlike most Central European countries, the Polish population continued to grow and the productivity of the still small-scale private peasant agriculture remained low. There was a serious problem of structural inflation, fuelled by the oil price shock in the 1970s and the consequent alignment of Soviet oil and gas prices to world price levels. Poland's industrial infrastructure remained outdated and uncompetitive. There was a vicious cycle of salaries being outstripped by inflation, which reached 300 per cent in 1982, and permanent shortages. In the 1970s Edward Gierek tried to maintain some economic growth by taking up massive Western loans, ultimately amounting to some $US 39.2 billion in 1989, the highest level of indebtedness in the whole Comecon bloc.

The key to any economic reform was to introduce market mechanisms, which would require 'realistic' rather than political (and hence artificially low) prices. But every attempt to raise prices led to serious political unrest and shook the regime to its foundations in 1956, 1970, 1971, 1976 and 1980. It had been shown repeatedly that, without political legitimacy, no tough economic reforms could succeed.

At the geopolitical level, Poland had always been a special case in the Eastern bloc, allowed a wide degree of internal latitude even by Stalin. But Poland was also more strategically important than Hungary or Czechoslovakia. By 1988 Mikhail Gorbachev had been in power in the Soviet Union for three years. In April 1988 an agreement had even been signed on the withdrawal of Soviet troops from Afghanistan. But although the Soviet Union had itself embarked on radical internal reforms which were already having external consequences, still no one could accurately predict the likely Soviet response to radical political change in central Europe. It might now tolerate some change, but how much? Obviously it would support and even encourage some *peristroika-* and *glasnost*-style reform, but Poland was already well beyond that and almost always had been. For Poland such reforms were 'no big deal', and thus any reform in Poland inevitably meant going beyond the Gorbachev reforms, radical though these undoubtedly were in the Soviet context. Poland would be leading, not following, the Soviet example. Would this be acceptable?

No one could know where Moscow's bottom line would be drawn. Would it be on the issue of Warsaw Pact membership or would it be on the issue of the leading role of the party? Historical evidence pointed in different directions. Sometimes, as had been the case with Austria and Finland in the late 1940s and early 1950s, ideological issues had been secondary. In Hungary and Czechoslovakia in the 1950s and the 1960s it was far from clear which concern had been the more important in motivating Soviet intervention. Moscow had also always been under pressure from the hardline communist leaderships in the GDR, Czechoslovakia, Bulgaria and Hungary. For these parties, ideological control had been the central issue, even if it hadn't been for Moscow.

Thus on the basis of past experience – insofar as that remained relevant and could be analysed accurately – the decision-makers in Warsaw had to factor into their calculations the likely reaction of a changing and increasingly unpredictable Soviet leadership. Nor should it be forgotten that the Moscow factor was always an instinctive point of reference for loyal communists, to an extent that is hard for Westerners to understand.

A simple summary of Jaruzelski's options in 1988/89 is set out in Table 4.1.

It should be stressed that these were not simply untried theoretical options. All of them, except full pluralism (option 6) had been tried with varying degrees of success, either in Poland or elsewhere in Central Europe after 1944, some if only for short periods of time.

Wladyslaw Gomoulka came to power on the wave of post-Stalinist change in Poland after 1956. In this first period he introduced carefully controlled and party-led economic and political reforms, with the reluctant consent of Moscow (option 2.2). In the later, more conservative period of his leadership he ceased to be a reformer and sought to defend the *status quo* by all available means (option 1). This then led directly to the first Gdansk riots in 1970 as Gomoulka had ignored the accumulating economic and political problems. (The *status quo* had also been the preferred option of the post-1968 Czechoslovak leadership.)

Table 4.1 Jaruzelski's options in 1988/89

		Advantages	Disadvantages
1.	The *status quo*	Would avoid political change. Moscow would not intervene	Would not resolve economic problems and would not be *actively* supported by Moscow in the 1980s
2.	Party-led (and hence limited and controlled) economic liberalisation	Would avoid political change and resolve economic problems	Would not create legitimacy and therefore might not work
2.2	Party-led (and hence limited and controlled) economic and political liberisation	Moscow's reaction unpredictable. If the reforms created legitimacy then Moscow might be supportive	The reforms might escape control, in which case Moscow would be against them
3.	Authoritarian non-ideological regime	Probably an effective short-term arrangement which might force change against PZPR vested interest. Some conservative legitimisation	No long-term domestic or Western legitimacy. Moscow's likely reaction hard to guage
4.	Power sharing	Legitimising control, but what would Moscow think?	Could it be controlled in the long term?
5.	Controlled pluralism	Legitimising long-term role for PZPR	Could it be controlled? How would Moscow respond?
6.	Full pluralism	Legitimising transfer and problem solving	It would eliminate the PZPR's leading role, and Moscow would almost certainly be opposed

Edward Gierek, who succeeded Gomoulka as first secretary of the Central Committee of the PZPR, preferred to concentrate on economic solutions without any accompanying political reforms (option 2.1). This approach failed because the envisaged reforms involved tough measures which lacked political legitimacy. The same option, pursued with greater flexibility, was more successful under Kádár in economically stronger Hungary. Jaruzelski himself initiated a form of 'Bonapartist' military rule in Poland in 1981 after the imposition of martial law (option 3). He was tempted to repeat this on a broader base in the late 1980s. (An even less salubrious example was that of Conducator Ceausescu in Romania.) A form of power sharing (option 4) had been developing between Solidarnosc and the PZPR in the period between the Gdansk strikes in the summer of 1980 and the imposition of martial law in 1981. In the immediate postwar period (1944–48), there had been limited forms of political pluralism (option 5) throughout the region, especially in Hungary and Czeschoslovakia, through communist-dominated, multiparty coalitions of national unity which preceded full communist control.

Through what prism did the Jaruzelski view the options available to him? Certainly his own experiences and character were relevant. He had to take into account the political and social peculiarities of Poland (particularly the role of the Church) and he knew that, as a special case, Poland had a certain, unspecified margin for manoeuvre. He had to try to calculate the probable reaction of the Soviet Union, and this meant that he had not only to monitor the changes taking place there but also to try and predict the likely outcome of them. (He was to get to know Mikhail Gorbachev very well and, perhaps revealingly, Gorbachev maintained that Jaruzelski was the Eastern European leader with whom he got on best.)[4]

Jaruzelski knew that conditions were not the same as they had been in 1956 or 1968, but equally he could not have imagined the extraordinarily rapid train of events which would be triggered by the fall of the Berlin Wall in the autumn of 1989. He had also, to a degree unprecedented in communist Europe, to take into account forces and factors outside the Polish and international communist world.

At the same time, although he may have become a hate figure for the opposition, its more realistic elements saw that he could be a valuable objective ally for them. Indeed the realists saw that Jaruzelski could be used to bring about and accelerate full pluralism precisely by providing reassurance to hardliners in the PZPR and to Moscow, hopefully until it was too late to reverse the process.

In the late 1990s, with all the sea changes which have taken place in former alliances, the bitter feuding in Solidarnosc, which ultimately destroyed the movement and its most emblematic figure, Lech Walesa, and the return to power of the reformed communists, there has been a tendency uncritically to weave into the flow of Polish history a consensual legend around Jaruzelski, as if he had in his own way been a part of the Polish revolution of 1989 as much as the opposition leaders. But that, like the demonisation of his role in 1981, is too simple a view of this complex and contradictory figure.

Jaruzelski's transition

In effect, in best pragmatic fashion Jaruzelski tested all of the possible options open to him, trying and discarding them until one that would work had emerged. He tested the limits of the possible; not excluding even a strategy of coexistence with a tamed or chastened Solidarnosc and civil society. This might have been achieved through a permanent redistribution of power, in which the party would retain its formal leading role and act as the guardian of Poland's geopolitical position. Ideally, such an approach even held open the possibility of the party acquiring a breathing space to recover at least some of its former dominance. But by 1988, as hinted in the previous section, it was no longer a case of Jaruzelski harnessing Solidarnosc to his purpose but, increasingly, the reverse. Solidarnosc would no longer serve him; he would serve Solidarnosc.

The various options set out in Table 4.1 above perhaps somewhat misleadingly appear as a continuum, seamlessly interconnected, the one with the other. However it is important to understand that in the perceptions of virtually all the actors at the time, including Jaruzelski and the Solidarnosc leaders, full pluralism (option 6) did not represent a point on a smooth continuum but rather a clear and apparently impossible rupture. As we now know with the benefit of hindsight, this perception was incorrect; pluralism too, had, simply become part of the continuum, no longer representing a rupture or a qualitative leap, but simply requiring a conscious decision. Hence, opting for power sharing or controlled pluralism (options 4 and 5) no longer represented an end point and actually could open the way to full pluralism, just as hardliners had always feared.

Despite an initial wave of arrests and repression, the *status quo ante-*1980 (option 1) was never a serious option. Even under martial law, repression had been relative and certainly did not crush or wholly eliminate civil society, as the far fiercer tsarist and Nazi repressions had done. By 1988 there was a general wind of change in the air and even the toughest hardliners must have begun to suspect that they might yet have to account for their actions.

General Jaruzelski, like many a political leader in the military arena, might instinctively have preferred some form of authoritarian and non-ideological regime (option 3). It was certainly too late for any party-led economic and/or political liberalisation (options 2.1 and 2.2), since such limited reforms would have been unlikely to resolve the escalating Polish crisis. Furthermore, partial liberalisation could well have encouraged confrontation and might even have led to Soviet intervention if the situation had become uncontrollable. The consequences of the 1981 declaration of martial law had shown Jaruzelski that the advantages of an authoritarian response could only be short term. Such a regime would enjoy no legitimacy in the West and Jaruzelski could not know how Moscow – which seemed to be moving away from more authoritarian models – might react. In short, by 1988 the authoritarian option was no longer available; a bigger gamble would be required.

In any case, by 1988 a type of Bonapartist, authoritarian economic reform, bypassing the party, had also failed.[5] There were numerous and indeed paradoxical reasons for this, in some ways reminiscent of the problems which Gorbachev was unable to resolve in the Soviet Union. In modern societies the existence of effective, responsible and reasonably legitimate intermediate structures between a powerful individual leader and society is a precondition of successful governance. But by 1981 the PZPR was a broken reed. It was losing membership, commitment and its former relative effectiveness. It was therefore tempting to bypass it or counterbalance it with other actors. In the immediate aftermath of martial law it indeed looked as if this would be the preferred path of Jaruzelski, with echoes of that very Polish figure, another socialist and nationalist general, Marshal Josef Pilsudski. But Polish society had changed substantially and, his lack of charisma apart, Jaruzelski could never have played the same role as Pilsudski who, although always a controversial figure, was nevertheless generally recognised as the father of the nation. Jaruzelski would never have been able to claim remotely equivalent legitimacy.

Although contact with the old Solidarnosc leadership, especially Lech Walesa, was completely taboo in the early 1980s, efforts were nevertheless made to reopen lines of communication with various civil groups on the fringes of Solidarnosc, and above all with the Catholic Church (which, now under Cardinal Glemp, had never burnt its bridges with the regime and remained available as a potential moderating force). But this approach could go nowhere because the old Solidarnosc leadership retained its attraction to the Polish people. No other group was ready or able to provide the legitimation of tough economic measures that Jaruzelski needed. The gradual realisation, as

1988 turned to 1989, that the direct threat of Soviet intervention, though not yet totally excluded, was receding encouraged the Polish people to be less apprehensive about the sort of political signals they sent out.

On 29 November 1988 Jaruzelski appealed directly to the people, seeking their approval through a referendum on a package of economic and political reforms. But what was on offer was too little too late for this strategy to work, especially with a more mature Solidarnosc waiting in the wings. The message was simultaneously ambiguous and unambiguous. With the economy continuing to deteriorate and no political solution likely, the PZPR Central Committee proposed a package of economic reforms which linked greater economic freedom for enterprises, a drastic increase in prices, a wage freeze and tight monetary policy together with a set of timid political reforms involving the creation of a consultative senate composed of representatives of local authorities and several other relatively minor measures. The electoral code required a majority of the electorate to approve a referendum. The turnout was only 67 per cent, even though voting was compulsory. Sixty-nine per cent of those voting approved the political reforms and 64 per cent the economic reforms, but this was only respectively 46 per cent and 42 per cent of the electorate. Consequently, the referendum was lost.[6]

Among the paradoxical causes of the failure of the attempted Bonapartist and referendum solutions was the simple fact that Polish society was no longer what it had been in the 1920s. Ironically, much of the change had been brought about by forty years of communist rule. The Poland of the 1980s was a younger, more mobile, more open, more critical and better educated nation. It was more urban, less rural and less traditionally Catholic. All in all, it was a less monolithic and less obedient society. Equally the process of *glasnost* and *peristroika* in the Soviet Union was also having an impact on Polish thinking and on the national psyche. The creation of a limited but real, and by past standards, significant consumer society in Poland, together with the bitter lessons of the destructiveness of Polish romantic heroism and the experience of Poland's Hungarian and Czech neighbours, had led to an uneasy and in historical terms quite new 'self-limitation' in Polish demands that had already begun to be evident in the first Solidarnosc period.

These more modest expectations were not something that the PZPR could easily designate as 'counter-revolution', threatening both its formal monopoly position and Poland's postwar alliances, but rather represented a desire for a pragmatic form of coexistence and *de facto* power sharing with the regime. This was an elastic and pragmatic concept. Expectations could expand and contract as conditions changed. *Glasnost*, in particular, offered a chance significantly to expand the horizons of reform. Without being able completely to discount the possibility of Soviet intervention, that traditional fear, so cynically exploited by the party and indeed by Jaruzelski himself in 1981, was losing its power. Fewer and fewer Poles believed that reform might provoke an interventionist Soviet response. On the contrary, it seemed increasingly as if it was the hardline Central European leaders who were out of step with Soviet thinking, as Gorbachev brutally illustrated with his famous 1989 admonition to the old dinosaurs in the DDR leadership that 'History will punish those who come too late'. By now it was Polish society and its reformers who could legitimately claim to be in the vanguard of history, and not the party leaders.

The shock of martial law was a rapidly diminishing asset. In the circumstances of the Poland of the late 1980s, neither the discredited party nor an authoritarian leader nor even the Catholic Church alone could carry sufficient conviction to get Polish society to accept tough economic reform. Similarly, the 1988 referendum had failed because its political component was quite simply an inadequate counterweight to the painful, if necessary, economic reforms it proposed. Put another way, the Polish people might have been prepared to accept the imposition of some economic austerity by Solidarnosc, but they certainly would not do so from the hated communist leadership, whose abuse of power and mismanagement were universally blamed for Poland's parlous condition. With the possible exception of a very brief period in 1981, Jaruzelski neither could nor would seek to disassociate himself from the party and its apparatus enough to make an alternative strategy work. (It was Gorbachev, more than any Central European leader, who 'ran' against the party.)

Thus Jaruzelski did not, in terms of how he sought to govern, make any radical departures from his predecessors, though there were occasional weak signals in that direction. But these were too timid and too short-lived to create the necessary dynamics for change. Did Jaruzelski want to bypass the PZPR, reform it or restore it? Or did he perhaps have no alternative concept other than that of attaching those independent actors that existed – the Church, individual reformers and eventually even Solidarnosc – to the project of limited reform and especially economic reform?

So by 1988 all of these approaches had failed, or at least had not produced any dramatic breakthrough, and time was not on Jaruzelski's side. Delay, perhaps a useful instrument in 1981, could have proved fatal in 1988. Jaruzelski was left with only one option: to reopen communications with Solidarnosc. Here too he could not wait too long. A new generation of more radical union activists was emerging which might soon reject the caution of the generation that had learned pragmatic lessons from the 1980/81 experience.

In 1988, when the rest of Central Europe seemed calm and the old geopolitical realities still seemed constant, Jaruzelski may well legitimately have believed that a dialogue with the opposition could be controlled and would not lead to radical change. He may have also believed that he could still win a race against time, for he and his reform group believed that the elections agreed under the Magdalenka round table formula would produce a result that would leave them with sufficient room for manoeuvre and force Solidarnosc to assume a degree of responsibility within a power-sharing arrangement that could be controlled. Jaruzelski's rueful comment on the election results that 'our experts had got it all wrong' confirms this interpretation of his probable strategic thinking (Duplan and Giret, 1994, p. 538).

In the 1988/89 period Jaruzelski often appeared a mysterious, vacillating, indecisive figure who had no clear game plan. Indeed in the early phases of renewed contact between Lech Walesa and the regime in the person of Jaruzelski's close confidant, Interior Minister General Kiczczak, Jaruzelski himself seemed reticent and absent from the scene. Did he have doubts or did he deliberately keep his distance? The general was a realist, and reaction to the imposition of the economic reform package, despite the referendum result and renewed waves of strikes in August 1988, had convinced him that he must act. Quite naturally he wanted to go the last mile in convincing a reluctant party only when he could be sure that Solidarnosc was prepared to take part in a round table.

When this was clear, he did go before the tenth plenum on 18 January 1989 and put his position on the line. Where necessary he did intervene to move the process forward.[7] He forced the party to agree to the legalisation of Solidarnosc and to the organisation of pluralistic elections. Speed was now of the essence. The round table that opened formally on 6 February and concluded on 5 April 1989 was presented with an insistent government demand for elections as early as June 1989. Solidarnosc was extremely fearful of this tactic, for it felt that it would have insufficient time to organise itself and could lose an early election. This was clearly Jaruzelski's hope – that early elections would produce a weak and compromised Solidarnosc.

Jaruzelski's legacy: how will history see him?

Jaruzelski sees his career as a coherent whole. For him, the two key decisions he took on his watch – the imposition of martial law and the opening up of the Magdalenka round table process – were not separate, contradictory decisions, but inextricably linked. He continues to insist that the second could not have happened without the first. The introduction of martial law was more than an immediate necessity in the situation of 1981. It was, more than the lesser evil, the only alternative in an immediate crisis. It was also a Polish solution. Jaruzelski has argued that the introduction of martial law 'ensured us the possibility of sovereign action and, above all, of continuing economic and social reforms' (Jaruzelski, 1996, p. 499). Weighing the alternatives, he has argued that 'under any other alternative, Poland would have lost everything. With martial law it lost, but did not lose all possibilities. These remained open for the future' (ibid.) He went on to argue that martial law was at that time best for Poland, for the USSR and for the West. Here he is without doubt right. Perhaps over-egging the pudding, he even argued that in the longer term it was best for Solidarnosc, which on its own admission was neither ready nor willing to assume power at that time. Hence he drew his paradoxical conclusion that 'Solidarnosc only finally won because it lost then'. Opinion polls both before and after 1989 showed that in December 1991, well after the fall of communism, 56 per cent of the Polish people agreed that the introduction of martial law had been justified, thereby apparently supporting Jaruzelski's analysis (ibid., p. 445).

To what extent is Jaruzelski's *ex-post* analysis credible? In his memoirs he appears to turn himself almost into a closet supporter of Solidarnosc, more lucid even than their own leadership. Though never explictly stated, this would be to go too far. Moreover, sceptics would argue that this analysis consistently enables him retrospectively to justify martial law as part of the tortuous path to the Magdalenka round table. The truth must lie somewhere in between. Jaruzelski was a patriotic leader of transition who found himself managing change in a far broader context of unpredictable change. It is perhaps not by chance that Jaruzelski's stock has risen in Poland since 1989 and that he has won the respect of some of the Solidarnosc opposition's most radical figures, such as Adam Michnik and Jacek Juron.

He is surely right when he argues that by the time he became prime minister there were desperately few options open to him. He was caught between Moscow and an overconfident Solidarnosc leadership. He could not broker a deal that would satisfy all those concerned: Solidarnosc, the Kremlin and the hardliners in Prague and East Berlin, as well of course as his own PZPR, army and security police. No compromise that would have satisfied Solidarnosc would have been accepted by the Kremlin nor, indeed by the PZPR at that time. In his own analysis, he notes that this was precisely what became possible in 1989, but that this

> was the result of a long process ... 1981 – that was quite simply a different time. ... confrontation was inevitable. Solidarnosc was simply pressing forward too radically. Opposition from the Party, administration, security forces and the army was certain ... the changes demanded by the opposition were simply not acceptable to the Warsaw Pact Allies of Poland (Jaruzelski, 1996, p. 448).

But is Jaruzelski right when he argues that, beyond this immediate necessity, martial law made 1989 possible as nothing else would have done and, more than that, enabled him to pursue the path that he would have liked to have been able to follow in 1981?

The answer must be both 'yes' and 'no'. Certainly the very particular form of martial law and, indeed, its objective moderation did freeze the situation internally and externally. It did buy time until Gorbachev came to power in Moscow (though nobody could have foreseen the scale and the scope of the reforms he would ultimately oversee), by which point Solidarnosc had also matured in the underground and was moving towards greater realism. Jaruzelski is also no doubt correct when he affirms that martial law enabled him to eliminate both the radical wing of Solidarnosc and his own party conservatives, both of whom were opposed to his tentative efforts at reform. He was effectively able to offer to Gorbachev an ideal laboratory for *perestroika*, better indeed than the USSR itself. This had become necessary because all other options except some form of controlled or full pluralism (options 5 and 6 in Table 4.1) had been tried and had failed.

What is much less certain is whether Jaruzelski, Gorbachev or the similar Hungarian reformists around Poszgay envisaged let alone supported the end result, which was a dramatic shift from versions of controlled pluralism (option 5) as they first emerged in the Polish

Magdalenka round table agreement to the full pluralism of option 6. However it is not inconceivable that Jaruzelski alone among communist reformers, coming as he did from the most anticommunist and anti-Soviet country of the Eastern bloc and one which alone actually had experience of an organised opposition outside the party, did indeed at least contemplate this possibility, as he said he did, and accept that risk – for Poland.

Retrospectively he at least saw himself as a screen between the pressures coming from the Soviet Union and hardline communist leaders such as Husák, Honecker and Kádár and the Polish people, and as a pragmatist who was in a certain sense above politics, able to seek a middle way between the extremist wings both of Solidarnosc and the PZPR. That, in his own view, was justification for the policies which made him unpopular, first with Solidarnosc in 1981 and then with his own party in 1989. There is undoubtedly a sense in which these *ex-post* justifications have the quality of a plea in mitigation or even of a self-fulfilling prophesy, particularly because he did experiment with many other options, but this should not necessarily lead to the outright rejection of Jaruzelski's self-analysis.

How should Jaruzelski now be assessed? He was long a hate figure in Poland. Ultimately he succeeded in being almost equally disliked by dissidents and hardline communists. This author must admit that he began this chapter strongly opposed to Jaruzelski, but analysis of the latter's career and avowed motives have brought him to a much less virulent view. In this context it is interesting that some leading dissidents of the 1980s, such as Adam Michnik, a key Solidarnosc activist and MP, have now come to hold a grudging respect for the general, seeing him almost as a tragic figure. Jaruzelski remains a complex and ambivalent personality, the product of a complicated and tragic period in East European history. Like many figures from that period, Jaruzelski was subject to competing claims for loyalty – Church, army, communism, fatherland – and their underpinning ideological and ethical frameworks.

In Jaruzelski's mind the one constant theme running through his actions was patriotism, and if this is accepted, then his own analysis of the events of the 1980s seems plausible; simply that he did what he did for his country within the constraints which existed at that time. Arguably the restraint he showed in the early 1980s avoided a Soviet backlash which might even have prevented a young moderniser like Mikhail Gorbachev from rising to the general secretaryship of the Soviet Communist Party in 1985. This may be how history finally comes to judge Wojciech Jaruzelski, but many Poles and commentators continue to regard him in a far more negative way. Noting this ambiguity is perhaps as far as one can get in assessing this complex and ambivalent figure who has so marked recent Polish history.

Wojciech Jaruzelski: chronology

1923, 6 July	Wojciech Jaruzelski was born in the village of Dobrowa Wielka in the Lublin district in eastern Poland. His parents were local gentry and devout and active Catholics.
1933–39	Attended a Jesuit gymnasium (grammar school) in Warsaw.
1941–43	Deported to the USSR. Worked as a labourer. Officers school at Ryazan in Siberia.
1943	Joined General Bering's (communist) army and fought his way through to Poland in 1945. Snow-blinded in the campaign.
1945–47	Career officer. Active role in destruction of Home Army (non-communist underground) guerrilla remnants.
1948–56	Various positions in the army: tactical planning staff, head of the Military Academy.
1956	Promoted to general, becoming Poland's youngest general.
1957–60	Commander of 12th Motorised Division.
1960–65	Chief political commissioner.
1965–68	Chief of staff of the army.
1968	Appointed defence minister
1970	Morally complicit in orders for troops to fire on demonstrators against price rises at Gdansk. At least 30 killed.
1971	Full Politburo member – Sejm deputy.
1981, February	Prime minister.
1981, October	First secretary of the PZPR.
1981, 13 December	Declared martial law and outlawed Solidarnosc.
1983, July	Lifted martial law.
1988, 29 November	Held referendum on economic and social reforms.
1989, 10 January	Went before 10th plenum to argue for opening round table
1989, 6 February – 5 April	Magdalenka round table
1989, 19 July	Elected president by the semi-democratic Sejm and Senate.
1990, 22 December	Stepped down after Walesa was elected president.

Notes

1 The PZPR, the United Polish Workers Party, was the ruling Communist

Party and held power in Poland from 1948 until 1989. It was formed out of the forced merger of the Communist and Socialist Parties.

2 For detailed descriptions of events and analyses of the motives of both Jaruzelski and the Solidarnosc leaders, see Duplan and Geret (1994), especially pp. 511–15, 529–35 and 536–8.

3 For an analysis of recent Polish history see Korbonski (1992).

4 Jaruzelski was 'probably [Gorbachev's] most trusted East European ally' (Garton Ash, 1993, p. 123).

5 It is noteworthy that Jaruzelski's first speech justifying martial law on 13 December 1981 was purely nationalistic and non-ideological. It does not mention socialism or the party at all. The speech is quoted in full in Duplan and Giret (1994), pp. 361–3. Garton Ash argued that 'In Poland, the Jaruzelski regime has entirely abandoned ideological self-justification ... the defence of Martial Law was conducted in almost entirely non-ideological terms' (Garton Ash 1983, p. 238).

6 On the referendum, see Bogdan (1990), pp. 567–8.

7 'It was Jaruzelski who on several occasions managed to cut through stalemated positions and rescue the negotiations from collapse' (Korbonski, 1992, p. 272).

References

Bogdan, H. (1990) *L'Histoire de l'Europe* (Paris: Perret).

Duplan, C., and U. Giret (1994) *Les Insoumis, 1968–1991* (Paris: Editions Seuil Mémoire).

Garton Ash, Timothy (1991) *The Uses of Adversity: Essays on the Fate of Central Europe* (Cambridge: Granta Books).

Garton Ash, Timothy (1993) *In Europe's Name* (London: Jonathan Cape).

Held, J. (1992) *A History of Eastern Europe in the Twentieth Century* (New York: Colombia University Press).

Jaruzelski, Wojciech (1996), *Hinter den Türen der Macht* (German edition of Jaruzelski's memoirs, originally published in Polish in 1992).

Korbonski, A. (1992) 'Poland 1918–1990', in Held, op. cit.

Neil Kinnock

[T]he task of reforming a democratic socialist party is one that
should never be referred to in the past tense
(Kinnock, 1984, p. 545)

From romantic to revolutionary to modernist. William Morris gazes over Neil
Kinnock's shoulder towards ... a Blairite future? (*Copyright © Andrew Wiard,*
Report)

5
Neil Kinnock: Loyalist Reformer

Martin Westlake

[T]he task of reforming a democratic socialist party is one that should
never be referred to in the past tense
(Kinnock, 1984, p. 545)

Two poignant images encapsulate the domestic political achievements of the Right Honourable Neil Gordon Kinnock. The first was his leader's speech to the 1985 Labour Party conference, in Bournemouth, when he turned on the 'grotesque chaos' of Liverpool's Labour Council, which had been reduced to 'hiring taxis to scuttle around a city handing out redundancies to its own workers' (Kinnock, 1992, p. 91). He thus signalled his intention to do serious battle with the extreme left, entryist Militant Tendency, which had threatened to render the party forever unelectable. The second took place in the early morning of 2 May 1997, as New Labour's extraordinary general election victory rolled over the Tory shires. Prime minister-elect Tony Blair was nearing the end of his slow, flashgun-lit procession through a rally on London's South Bank when he was greeted by the man who, in November 1984, had given him his first experience of front bench politics, Neil Kinnock. The two men embraced emotionally and then moved on; Blair to acknowledge the enthusiasm of the crowd, Kinnock to melt into it.

The full extent of Kinnock's political legacy is now clear. When he became leader of the opposition in 1983 he had long-since realised that wide-ranging reforms would be required if the party were ever to be elected again. The 1987 general election defeat demonstrated that radical policy change would be required to re-establish Labour's relevance to the mainstream of the British electorate. The subsequent policy review involved an at times painful process of self-appraisal and led Kinnock gradually to alter some of his most firmly held views, particularly on defence. He lost personal friends and was accused of denaturing himself and adopting a distant and authoritarian approach ('tolerance,' it was argued, 'had taken second place to the will to win' – McSmith, 1996, p. 62). He had consistently believed that 'idealism is the energy of socialism' but that 'realism is the means to carry it out', (Kinnock, 1983b) and he was convinced that the party would be best served by addressing itself to the evolving perceptions and requirements of the electorate at large.

It is now widely recognised that these policy reforms laid the foundations for Tony Blair's 1997 success and the Labour Party's new-found electoral appeal. Indeed, as Blair has acknowledged at every party conference since he was elected leader in 1994, Labour could not have hoped to win in 1997 without Kinnock's many achievements as leader. As he looks about him today, Kinnock can see the modern social-democratic party whose creation he encouraged and the ministers whose careers he did so much to advance. Meanwhile, the man Denis Healey described as 'One of the tragic heroes of politics' (Healey interview) is ensconced as a European commissioner in Brussels, almost entirely excluded from his own creation.

To what extent did Kinnock initiate the process of change which ultimately led to the Blair administration of 1997? Was he simply the instrument of changes which would have occurred whoever had been leader? Had Kinnock known of his fate, would he still have sought the leadership and devoted nine years to the drudgery of reform?

From Tredegar to Westminster

Kinnock was born in March 1942 in Tredegar, a South Wales steel and coal town. His father had been a miner before being disabled by dermatitis, his mother a district nurse. An only child and the object of great parental devotion, he never personally knew poverty but learned of its effects from his parents and wider family. Although his parents were determined that he should escape the classic valley destiny of manual labour, Kinnock nevertheless grew up deeply imbued with the romantic and political lore of the Welsh mining community.

His parents were staunch Labour voters but were not party members. Labour Party politics came to Kinnock at the age of fifteen, when he started talking politics with a local miner and Labour councillor, Bill Harry, who encouraged Kinnock to attend a local discussion group and recruited him to the party. It was in the meetings of the discussion group that he consolidated his confidence for taking on and winning arguments. A Tredegar contemporary 'always knew he was going to be a politician ... that was all he was interested in' (Batten interview).

Kinnock passed his eleven-plus and won entry to the prestigious Lewis School for Boys in the next valley. Strict academic life bored him and he had to retake his 'O' levels. However he did sufficiently well at 'A' level to be accepted at University College, Cardiff, for a degree in industrial relations and history. It was there that Kinnock's political interests and gifts were consolidated, particularly through the University Debating Society and the Students' Union, and he rapidly developed into a charismatic and combative orator whose main political interests were the Socialist Society and the Anti-Apartheid Movement. He also met his future wife, Glenys Parry, an attractive and politically active undergraduate with an even more authentic Labour Party pedigree. The two became a strong political team.

Jim Callaghan, then a local MP and for whom Kinnock campaigned in the 1964 general election, remembers him as an 'exuberant, cheerful, energetic, enthusiastic university politician'. But also as 'an undirected missile, and a very powerful one at that. He was an explosive force, a young man of great promise' (Callaghan interview). It was also at Cardiff that Kinnock first displayed reformist zeal, successfully campaigning in 1965 for the presidency of the Students' Union on the slogans 'a mandate for change' and 'Kinnock for Efficiency, Initiative, Approachability, Experience.' Kinnock's presidency witnessed a series of constitutional and administrative reforms, although it was also increasingly dogged by student apathy and minority opposition. A fractious row involving both him and Glenys (who was chairwoman of the Cardiff branch of the National Union of Students) ultimately led to his resignation. This must have been a critical formative influence on the future Labour leader. For the first time Kinnock experienced the inertia confronting the reformer, and perhaps also saw the way in which apathy could enable well-organised cliques to capture strong points within an organisation.

In 1966 Kinnock began work as a Workers' Educational Association tutor-organiser, a job which involved travelling about South Wales and lecturing to mature students. Kinnock married Glenys (now also a teacher) in March 1967 and they set up house in Pontllanfraith, where they formed the kernel of a group of young Bevanites seeking to rejuvenate and modernise the local Bedwellty Labour Party. Over the next two years Kinnock made his name locally through his speaking abilities and his appearances on regional television. He became known for his charm, wit and enthusiasm. He was a hard-working canvasser, a great motivator and showed natural leadership powers. He was also undeniably ambitious.

When in February 1969 the Bedwellty MP, Harold Finch, suddenly announced that he would be standing down at the next election, the young Turks made a daring attempt for the position. Kinnock was the obvious candidate, and in the resulting cliff-hanger his oratorical gifts helped him to capture the nomination to one of the safest seats in Britain. He quickly set about introducing new procedures to the working practice of the local party and organised 'Chartist rallies' to enliven the constituency. In the June 1970 general election Kinnock was elected MP for Bedwellty with a 22 279 majority. He was just twenty-eight. The Neil Kinnock who arrived at Westminster in 1970 was a quintessentially Welsh politician. Virtually all of his political development had taken place in a small area of South Wales, stretching from Tredegar to Cardiff. His attentions would now increasingly turn to the party and the country as a whole.

From MP to party leader

In 1970 Labour found itself unexpectedly out of power and Kinnock has since spoken of the 'confusing and bewildering' experience of sitting on the opposition back benches (Jones, 1994, p. 29). Though able to make his mark with occasional flights of wit and oratory, his frustration was demonstrated by the 239 written questions he tabled during his first four years in the Commons. He was reelected in February 1974 with a 21 637 majority.

Labour was now in power, but the Harold Wilson of the 1974–6 period was a shadow of his 1964 incarnation, and Labour's majority, after the second October 1974 general election, remained small. Kinnock was decidedly on the left, a member of the Tribune Group, and as an early member of the Campaign for Labour Party Democracy was particularly supportive of calls to widen the franchise for the election of the party leader. He was an active anti-marketeer, antiracist campaigner and CND supporter. Over the next four years he consolidated his left-wing credentials, with occasional acts of rebellion against the Wilson and Callaghan governments, whilst simultaneously raising his public and party profile.

Moreover, with the exception of a brief early period as Michael Foot's private parliamentary secretary, Kinnock steered clear of the traditional political career ladder, turning down at least one offer of a junior ministerial post. This decision to keep clear of office was to prove a powerful part of his appeal in 1983.

During the 1970–9 period Kinnock won his spurs as a robustly independent backbencher on two particular issues, his approach to each of which was intimately bound up with his Welsh background. The first was membership of the European Economic Community (EEC). Kinnock's opposition to membership was pragmatic, being grounded primarily in the belief that it would damage Welsh economic interests (Drower, 1984, p. 32).

The second issue was devolution. Kinnock was an unwavering opponent of a policy which was vital to the minority 1974–9 Labour government because of its dependence on the support of minority parties, including the Scottish and Welsh nationalists. Kinnock's position earned him the wrath of the party hierarchy and put him in direct opposition to his friend and mentor, Michael Foot, who was now leader of the House with special responsibility for devolution: but it also confirmed him as a man of principle, and 'at last began to prove his capacity for the grind of politics' (Harris, 1984, p. 106). Moreover, unlike EEC membership:

> The referendum result was a clear vindication of Kinnock's long campaign: in neither Scotland nor Wales was there anywhere near the 40 per cent of the total electorate required to win. In Wales the majority was four to one against the establishment of an Assembly (Jones, 1994, p. 36).

Throughout the 1970s Kinnock also honed his speaking and journalistic skills. He was a frequent contributor to *Tribune* and the *Guardian* and became a regular fixture on television. His stock within the party steadily rose, particularly following a witty and confident performance at the October 1975 Tribune rally, and in 1978 he was elected to the NEC at the age of 36. But within a year Labour would lose a general election and be destined to remain out of office for the next 18 years.

Kinnock maintains that the defining moment for him came not in 1983 – though the experience of the party's at times comically shambolic campaign was seared into his memory – but in 1979. Kinnock saw the 1979 defeat as more than the simple swing of the electoral pendulum. He felt that something deeper was occurring – one of those occasional sea changes in British electoral politics which change the basic terms of the political debate.[1] It was, he realised, 'put up or shut up time' (LWT, 1992). On 18 June of the same year he was appointed shadow education spokesman. His decision to stand for election to the shadow cabinet signalled a first breaking of ranks with the left. It was 'the hinge upon which his career turned. It demonstrated that for Kinnock politics is not about striking heroic stances: it is about power' (Harris, 1984, p. 125). Although the education portfolio was an awkward brief, Kinnock consolidated his popularity in the party at the October 1979 Brighton conference with a rousing speech which won him a standing ovation. Later the same week he moved up to second place in the NEC elections. In February 1980 he warned the PLP that the economic situation would dictate what parts of the Thatcherite agenda a future Labour government might be able to reverse. As two very different observers noted, Kinnock was 'starting to speak as though he might one day be in government' (Owen, 1991, pp. 430–1).[2]

It was at this moment, with the Labour Party consigned to impotent opposition, that the frustrated and increasingly fractious Bennite left and the Campaign for Labour Party Democracy sought retribution for what they saw as the cumulative slights of the right-wing Wilson and Callaghan leaderships. The dismal story of the fratricidal struggles which followed needs no repeating here. As Kinnock himself described the period:

> In the years between our defeat in 1979 and our defeat in 1983 Labour was increasingly seen to be a party slipping towards impossibilism, succumbing to fads, riven by vicious divisions, speaking the language of sloganised dogma – and usually voicing it in the accents of menace. It was almost as if sections of the party measured the purity of their socialism by the distance which they could put between it and the minds of the British people (Kinnock, 1994, p. 535).

The next two years saw, in rapid succession, the introduction of mandatory re-selection for MPs, Jim Callaghan's resignation, the election of Kinnock's old mentor, Michael Foot, as the new leader, changes to the rules governing leadership elections and the drafting of the party's electoral manifestos, and the departure of David Owen, Shirley Williams and William Rodgers to set up a new Social Democratic Party. On 2 April 1981 Tony Benn announced that he would be challenging the incumbent deputy leader of the party, Denis

Healey. It would be the first leadership election under the new rules. On 25 April 1981 Kinnock made a widely reported speech in which he warned the far left that, by expecting too much too soon from a future Labour government, it was indulging in fantasy. Over the summer Kinnock decided that he could not support Benn's bid. In an 18 September 1981 *Tribune* article he argued that 'by a tactically mistaken decision to contest the deputy leadership in 1981, Tony has significantly harmed the current standing and electoral opportunities of the Labour Party'. Kinnock and fifteen others subsequently backed the no-hope candidature of John Silkin in the first round and abstained in the second, narrowly depriving Benn of victory.[3] Kinnock's abstention was 'a turning-point in Labour's history' (Sopel, 1995, p. 75). It also consolidated his status as a potential candidate for the party leadership.

Benn's defeat did not quell the left's demands for radical reform. Over the next two years internecine warfare continued very publicly. Conservative popularity was meanwhile boosted by a successful conclusion to the 1982 Falklands War and an economic recovery. Margaret Thatcher called a general election for 9 June 1983. Labour's campaign was confused and incompetent, and the Conservatives romped home, taking 397 seats to Labour's 209: 'The working class had deserted in their millions, with fewer than 40 per cent of trades unionists and less than half the unemployed voting Labour' (Jones, 1994, p. 52).

Foot resigned as leader and Kinnock immediately became a favourite in the leadership race, not only because the new electoral college would favour him but also because he was genuinely popular among trades unionists. Roy Hattersley, Kinnock's strongest rival, was more popular among shadow cabinet members but was older and had served as a minister in the discredited 1974–9 Labour government. Kinnock luckily survived a spectacular car crash in the summer and his leadership campaign steadily strengthened. On 1 October 1983 he was elected leader, taking 71.3 per cent of the votes cast. Hattersley took just 19.3 per cent of the vote, but saw off a strong challenge from Michael Meacher to be elected deputy leader. The 'dream ticket' alliance of left and right had considerable symbolic significance and reflected the fact that the vast majority of Labour parliamentarians, trades unionists and party members desired party unity and a fresh political initiative. Neil Kinnock was 'young, radical, a great orator, full of life, full of hope and, perhaps most importantly of all, uncontaminated by membership of the Labour Government of 1974–79'

(Hattersley, LWT, 1992) He was widely perceived as an energetic moderniser from the left.

Kinnock's extraordinarily rapid rise to the leadership seemed perfectly to encapsulate Oprah Winfrey's saying that 'Luck is a matter of preparation meeting opportunity.' Put another way, 'To say that Kinnock's career has been lucky ... is a way of avoiding the need for explanation. If Kinnock has had a habit of being in the right place at the right time, this has been because he has put himself there' (Pimlott, 1995, pp. 130–1). Yet Kinnock could never have been considered a straightforward careerist. On the contrary, his early political career was dotted with occasions when he clearly acted with reference to his principles – or to what one commentator has called his 'gut'[4] – rather than his career interests; his opposition to devolution, for example, and his loyalty to Foot even when the latter had blundered politically, as he did during the February 1983 Bermondsey by-election campaign.

Leader of transition: diagnosis, methodology and constraints

1983: diagnosis

It was 'difficult to think of any campaign fought by a major party since the war that was more inept than Labour's in 1983' (Butler and Kavanagh, 1984, p. 274). During the campaign the party's poll support dropped from 36 per cent to 28 per cent – its lowest share of the vote since 1918. Kinnock experienced the organisational and presentational chaos at first hand, but he also subscribed to those analyses which argued that 'The election was lost not in the three weeks of the campaign but in the three years which preceded it' (Denis Healey, quoted in Butler and Kavanagh, 1984, p. 278). It had been a humiliating experience. As Kinnock exhorted the party immediately after his election to the leadership: 'remember how you felt on that dreadful morning of 10 June? Just remember how you felt then, and think to yourselves: "June the Ninth, 1983; never ever again will we experience that"' (Kinnock, 1992, p. 39). His private conclusion was that there would have to be 'profound changes in the policies and in the organisation of the Labour Party – not simply as ends in themselves but also as contributions to the change in the mentality of the Labour Party' (Kinnock, 1994, p. 536).

Kinnock came to the leadership with a rudimentary gameplan

worked out.[5] As *The Economist* speculated:

> Mr Kinnock's intention is to proceed by stages away from the more extreme manifesto commitments presented in June [1983]. His research team had already prepared the ground with a pre-conference document, 'Campaigning for a Fairer Britain', which is extraordinarily vague on policy on Europe, nuclear weapons, nationalisation and housing (*The Economist*, 8 October 1983).

Even before his election as leader, Kinnock had sought a less electorally disadvantageous stance with regard to EC membership. More attuned than his predecessors and successors to the potential of the European Parliament and of the British Labour contingent within it, he saw the forthcoming June 1984 European Assembly elections not only as Labour's next national electoral test, but also as an opportunity to demonstrate a *rélance* and to confirm the SDP–Liberal Alliance's position in third place. The policy of outright withdrawal espoused by the 1983 manifesto had contributed to Labour's image as being unrealistic, and Kinnock saw that the illogicality of fighting European elections on such a platform would be exposed, as it had been in the disastrous 1979 European elections (when the Conservatives won 60 seats to Labour's 17).

In a 15 September 1983 speech to the Socialist Group in the European Assembly (Luxembourg) he argued that 'withdrawal should be regarded as a last resort that is considered only if and when the best interests of the British people cannot be feasibly safeguarded by any other means' (Kinnock, 1983a, p. 2).[6] Later in the year, exploiting his authority as the new leader, Kinnock was able to ensure implicit acceptance of continued EC membership in *Campaigning for a Fairer Britain*. It was the first step on a long road which would end, in 1989, with Labour support for membership of the ERM and the fiscal orthodoxy which lay behind it.

In the same September 1983 Luxembourg speech, Kinnock told his continental socialist confrères that, in the wake of Labour's terrible defeat, there was a need for 'a great deal of serious re-thinking about organisation, presentation and, most of all, the direction of the Labour Party. It is a time to listen carefully to what the British people are saying and a time to learn from other Socialists' (Kinnock, 1983a, p. 2). These words, delivered before Kinnock became leader, effectively signalled all that he would set out to do over the next decade.

Methodology

Having diagnosed the party's ills, Kinnock set out to cure them by 'assembling the available assets and undertaking what would now be called the "re-engineering" of the enterprise with the purpose of producing electability' (Kinnock, 1994, p. 537). The 're-engineering' was to consist of structural and policy reform, the two governed by an underlying strategy and, necessarily, by short-term tactical considerations. On the structural side Kinnock:

- Gradually transformed Labour's 'management team' through key appointments, such as that of Larry Whitty as general secretary of the party and Peter Mandelson as head of communications, combining these with the leader's Private Office (particularly Charles Clarke, who served as 'chief fixer' throughout Kinnock's term as leader, and Patricia Hewitt), to create an able and loyal team which shared the overall reformist objective.
- Sought structural changes, such as an early form of one member one vote (OMOV) and joint policy committees intended respectively to enable the leader to appeal to a broader and more balanced party constituency, and to render the party more manageable and more coherent.
- Professionalised the party by concentrating far more on communications and polling skills (including the 1986 formation of the Shadow Communications Agency and the exploitation of communications experts such as Peter Mandelson, Philip Gould and Peter Kellner).[7]
- Gradually centralised power in the leader's office.
- Sought to construct a stable working majority on the NEC. Though it was not until 1989 that he had an assured majority, the breakthrough came in a crunch 29 September 1985 meeting when a 'torn apart' Michael Meacher decided to back Kinnock in refusing to commit a Labour government to paying retrospective compensation to miners who had suffered legal penalties in the 1984–5 strike.[8]
- Brought on a generation of able Labour parliamentarians who would not only act cohesively in opposition but could form the backbone of a Labour administration (this process was much accelerated after the 1987 defeat – Kinnock was a gifted political talent spotter, as the composition of the current Labour government shows).[9]

On the policy side, Kinnock knew that the party's policies would 'have to be altered in order to broaden and deepen the appeal of the Labour Party' (Kinnock, 1994, p. 539). As one commentator put it, 'socialism had to be reinterpreted to accommodate the new emphases on consumerism, individualism and choice' (Wintour, 1992, p. 27). Kinnock retrospectively divided policies into three categories:

- Those which could be changed without encountering major resistance, such as the party's policy on council house sales and its policy towards the European Community.
- Those which could probably be changed with 'greater effort and the right timing', such as the antagonism towards trade union ballots and the general policy on nationalisation.
- Those with 'particularly deep roots that were, in themselves, benchmarks of political disposition within the Labour Party' – chief among these was the issue of nuclear disarmament (Kinnock, 1994, p. 540).

Constraints

In setting out to achieve these reforms, Kinnock faced a number of constraints which governed the short- and medium-term tactics he was obliged to adopt.

The first was the simple problem of inertia within the party, which Kinnock once described as the 'supertanker problem' (Jones, 1996, p. 114). It took a long time to change direction, and a sharp movement could split the ship in two: 'without long preparation and a variety of actions to push and persuade people and organisations into changed positions, the status quo – or something worse than that – would have prevailed' (Kinnock, 1994, p. 536). Changing the party's policy on council house sales, for instance, took 'two years from my election as Leader. It was much too long – but at least it provided a working model for other changes' (ibid., pp. 541–2). To borrow a favourite phrase of François Mitterrand, he had to 'give time to time' and allow change to seep gently through, but – and here was the rub – the Conservative government was meanwhile enacting a radical policy agenda which was tugging the political centre further right and implied yet more change to make the Labour Party electable.

Besides those against change almost on principle, some parts of the Labour movement were suspicious of, or slow to see the need for, reform. An important part of Kinnock's job was, therefore, to explain

and to reassure: 'at all times I had to combine the process of adjust-
ment with perpetual reminders of the purpose of change' (ibid., p.
540). The result was an additional heavy charge on the leadership.

A second constraint was the burden of the past. The Labour movement was proud of its traditions, and in his quest for modernisation
Kinnock had to struggle against an instinctive attachment to the
symbols (the singing of the 'Red Flag', for example) and the culture of
the past. The Labour Party's conservatism was a phenomenon widely
remarked upon. It was a 'complex mix of assertiveness and defensive-
ness, of secular fragmentation and group loyalty, which has shaped
Labour's tradition and contributed to the paradoxical conservatism of
the labour movement' (Marquand, 1991, p. ix). An authentic product
of the movement, son of a miner and quintessential party man,
Kinnock had the advantage of affecting change from within,[10] but by
the same standards his insider status laid him open to charges of
betrayal in a way which would have been irrelevant to a middle-class
leader such as Tony Blair.

The third was continued internal division and the concomitant risk
of schism. The Jenkinsite right had already quit and risked acting as a
beacon to the disaffected centre-right. Hence the fight against
Militant had a triple objective and at times required very delicate
manoeuvering. First, it gave a strong message to the broader electorate
that the leadership was bent on rejecting extremism. Second, it
signalled to those on the right within the Party that they could and
should stay. Third, it sought to detach the 'soft' from the 'hard' left
and encourage it and the centre-right to coalesce.

For these reasons, Kinnock had to follow up the 1985 Bournemouth
speech with the agonised tedium of the creation of the National
Constitutional Committee, the hearings and the expulsions and the
innumerable NEC meetings – a period graphically described as 'grind-
ing years of raging obstinacy' (McSmith, 1996, p. 17). Justice – or
constitutional propriety – had to be seen to be done, but because it
required the hands-on involvement of Kinnock as a sort of 'chief pros-
ecutor' it amounted to another massive burden on the leadership.

The fourth were the exogeneous issues which arose throughout the
1980s, including the miners' strike, 'black sections' (a proposal from
the left to establish separate units of the party for non-white
members) and 'loonie left' local councils. Of these, the miners' strike
inflicted most damage on the Kinnock leadership. It frittered away his
'honeymoon period', making him seem weak and indecisive, and reinforced the image of Labour as being out of date. In private Kinnock

was ferociously critical of Scargill's strategy and later regretted not having taken an early public stance in favour of ballotting (Westlake, 1999), but here the collective leadership was still labouring under the burden of the past: 'The ghosts of the General Strike of 1926 were walking through the shadow cabinet room and our failure then was not a failure of judgement – we knew what was right – it was sentimentality' (Hattersley, LWT, 1992).

A fifth was the existence of the Liberal/SDP Alliance, which was to remain a potent threat, as a number of by-election gains, such as Greenwich (February 1987) and Glasgow Govan (November 1988), demonstrated.[11] More fundamentally, the attempted occupation of the electoral centre ground by the Alliance made it more difficult for Kinnock openly to espouse the sorts of policy changes necessary for his quest for renewed electability.[12]

The sixth constraint was the fact that 'there was no traditional or institutional means within the Party for the Shadow Cabinet or Parliamentary Labour Party to instigate such changes' (Jones, 1996, p. 114). Though he later regretted that he had not forced radical change through more rapidly, the truth was that Kinnock had to feel his way through the transition process – there was no precedent for what he intended to do.

The final constraint derived from the fact that Kinnock was chasing moving targets, particularly in two senses: the effects of the radical policy agenda which, thanks to their crushing majorities, the Thatcher administrations of the 1980s pursued at great speed; and the social, demographic and economic changes upon which that agenda was predicated and indeed encouraged. They were changes Kinnock increasingly understood.[13]

An early attempt at reform provided a salutory lesson on how Kinnock would have to proceed. In 1983 the new leader surveyed the 'limited assets' at his disposal and concluded that he must seek the support of the broader Labour Party membership as an enabling device, hence the attempt to establish 'a rudimentary system of one member one vote (OMOV) for the selection and re-selection of candidates in seats already held by Labour' (Kinnock, 1994, p. 537). But the move was defeated at the October 1984 party conference. Political analysts perceived a number of tactical errors: the leader had set personal popularity (a diminishing and unreliable asset) against entrenched interests; he had campaigned on two fronts (the left in the constituencies and the union block vote); and he had failed to count where the votes were (McSmith, 1996, p. 46). For Kinnock the defeat:

strongly confirmed my belief that change of all kinds would have to be pursued by very thorough and calculated means: it was clear that it would be essential to compile majorities for reforms in the Constitution or amendments to policy before even putting them for decision, whether to the NEC and its committees or to the National Conference. The reason was simple – the Leader of the Labour Party seeking reform and revival of the party simply could not afford to be defeated on any central issue' (Kinnock, 1994, p. 538).

1987 and beyond

Labour went into the 1987 election facing a Tory lead of more than ten points. 'It was to emerge the other side of polling day facing a 101–seat Tory majority. Labour had run an effective, modern and televisual campaign. Kinnock had not failed his party and indeed suddenly became its best asset. It was the defeat without excuses' (Wintour, 1992, p. 28). On the centre and right of the party, the gloomy conclusion was that organisational and presentational excellence were insufficient: 'you can't sell something that people don't want, however well you package it' (Gerald Kaufman, LWT, 1992). Kinnock had always presumed he would need to play a 'two innings match' (Kinnock, 1994, p. 543), but the scale of the 1987 defeat was a catalytic experience from which Kinnock concluded that nothing short of a complete overhaul of the party's policies would do if democratic socialism was 'to be as attractive, as beckoning and as useful to the relatively affluent and the relatively secure as it is to the less fortunate in our society' (Kinnock, quoted in McSmith, 1996, p. 66).

Kinnock therefore decided on 'a comprehensive policy review that was greater in scope, more ambitious in intention and more rigorous in application than the [existing] Joint Policy Committee system' (Kinnock, 1994, p. 543). Existing draft proposals were implemented with the creation of seven policy review groups. To ensure 'greater strategic coordination' each group's work was shadowed by a member of Kinnock's staff.[14] To add urgency to the process, Kinnock got the shadow communications agency to paint a grim picture of Labour and Britain in the 1990s. It argued that the party would progressively lose touch with society and become increasingly irrelevant to the electorate unless it changed (ibid., p. 546).

In 1988 Tony Benn challenged Kinnock for the leadership, encouraging Eric Heffer and John Prescott to challenge Roy Hattersley for the deputy leadership. Kinnock saw both challenges as huge irritants and unwelcome distractions.[15] But the subsequent crushing defeats for Benn and Prescott in particular (Kinnock won 88.6 per cent, Hattersley 66.8 per cent) consolidated Kinnock's leadership, rendered the far left largely irrelevant (though not to the media) and enabled the policy review process to proceed essentially unchallenged.

A key element in the review was Labour's defence policy. When elected leader, Kinnock had been a staunch unilateralist, but his views began to change in the 1985–6 period following the Gorbachev–Reagan summit in Reykjavik: 'It clinched my view that multilateralism was now so possible and unilateralism so unpopular that the policy change had to come' (23 December 1998 interview with the author). But Kinnock knew that this issue could easily split the party, as it had done in the past. Just as importantly, Labour's unilateralist stance had been singled out as a major vote loser and a failure to reform the party's defence policy would have undermined the review process. Kinnock's language was gradually transformed, and his attempts to signal change whilst simultaneously hiding it 'gave him an unfair reputation as a waffler' (Richards, 1998, p. 22). Whether unfair or not, these at times conflicting signals also led to controversy, the resignation of his shadow defence secretary, Denzil Davies, and an early setback at the 1988 conference (owing to the unions' block vote). But Kinnock persevered and, with considerable assistance from Gerald Kaufman, his shadow foreign affairs spokesman, was able to push a new multilateral approach. At the 9 May 1989 NEC meeting, which considered Kaufman's multilateralist policy paper, Kinnock said:

> Many in this room have protested and marched in support of nuclear disarmament. I have done that. But I have done something else: I have gone to the White House, the Kremlin, the Elysée, and argued the line for unilateral disarmament.... I have to tell you that I am not going to make that tactical argument for the unilateral abandonment of nuclear weapons without getting anything in return ever again (Jones, 1994, p. 127).

The NEC approved the switch by seventeen votes to eight, and on 2 October 1989, the new defence policy was approved by the party conference.

The policy review documents, the product of eighteen months' work, were published in May 1989 under the title *Meet the Challenge,*

Make the Change. The programme was hailed as one of the most comprehensive sets of proposals ever assembled mid-term by any British political party. Two major themes had emerged:

> First, intraparty political debate over the extent of public and private ownership was outdated; and second, the quality of public services should be improved by putting the needs of the user before those of the producer... The report came down in favour of private ownership and affirmed that a Labour government's task would be to stimulate a successful market economy and that it would intervene only where stimulation was not coming from market forces (Patrick Seyd in King, 1992).

Meet the Challenge, Make the Change remains an enduring testament to Kinnock's leadership. He 'drove the plan for the policy review through a sullen and uncertain conference, and it was his energy more than anything which drove the process forward over the next two years' (Sopel, 1995, p. 180). Kinnock realised the risk he was taking, in particular by opening himself and the party to charges of opportunism: but 'It was a risk that had to be taken. Not changing policy would have been wrong and tantamount to suicide' (23 December 1998 interview with the author).

There were to be two further policy documents before the next general election. *Looking to the Future*, published in May 1990, was intended as a sort of mini-manifesto. It notably included a commitment to the ERM and subsequently the party's long-standing commitment to full employment was dropped. The move was strongly criticised on the left, but Kinnock had 'made the argument for six years that asserting demands for full employment impressed no-one, least of all the unemployed' (23 December 1998 interview with the author). The second policy document, *Opportunity Britain* (May 1991), was basically a repackaged policy review. More structural changes to the party were also effected during the 1989–91 period, including further reductions in the power of the trades unions and the reselection of MPs on a one member one vote basis.

Had there been a general election in 1990, Labour might easily have won. The controversy over the Poll Tax had eaten deeply into the Conservative government's support and Thatcher's popularity. In the spring of 1990 two polls gave Labour more than fifteen points' lead and Kinnock at last overtook Thatcher in the voters' estimation of the leader best-equipped to be prime minister. In March 1990 Labour won its best by-election victory for 50 years, overturning a 14 000 Tory majority to take Mid Staffordshire.

But within two years the Conservatives had replaced Thatcher with John Major as leader and won a fourth successive election, and a strong school of thought developed within the Labour Party that Kinnock himself had become an electoral liability. The causes of the 9 April 1992 defeat were far more complex than a simple matter of the personal popularity of the party leaders. Nevertheless Kinnock, the dynamic and persevering moderniser, somehow came to be portrayed as an opportunistic electioneer who could easily revert to the 'old ways'. It took two more party leaders and another general election before the suspicion of Labour was finally overcome.

Achievement

Although a general election victory evaded Kinnock, his enduring achievement was to transform the 'impossibilist', faction-ridden, union-dominated Labour Party of the early 1980s into a leaner, forward-looking, social-democratic party relevant to a centre-left majority and capable of winning elections. In 1983 Labour had 'abandoned the centre ground of British politics and camped out on the margins, forlorn and useless, offering a miasma of extremism, dogmatism, intolerance and wilful elitism which put the hopes and dreams of ordinary people last' (Gould, 1998, p. 4). In particular it had 'failed to understand that the old working class was becoming a new middle class' (ibid.)[16] There was a real prospect of the party becoming marginalised, a shrinking party of declining areas and populations, with the Liberal–Social Democrat Alliance as the primary anti-Conservative force (McKibbin, 1997, p. 6).[17] But Kinnock both sensed that 'A new class of fairly unconservative people was emerging, and would go on emerging, partly thanks to Thatcher',[18] and through his reforms created the new Labour machine that was to enable Blair to take Labour to its biggest electoral landslide and realise his vision of the party as 'a broad coalition of those who believe in progress and justice, not a narrow, class-based politics, but a party founded on clear values, whose means of implementation changes with generations' (*Guardian*, 16 December 1998).

The post-Kinnock Labour Party was unrecognisable from that in any other period of the party's history – and not just the chaos of 1979–83. Its whole culture had changed. Kinnock exorcised the ghost of Ramsay

Macdonald and made the Labour Party, if not love, at least respect and obey its leader. The party's internal lines of conflict realigned and eventually blurred, with the marginalisation of the 'hard left' and the growing coalescence of the 'soft left' and the right, leading to the situation today, where former 'left wing' figures such as Clare Short, David Blunkett and Margaret Beckett serve in a Blair cabinet. Kinnock changed party policy as much if not more than any previous leader. Labour was converted to the market economy, Europe, the bomb and constitutional reform. The party was more democratic than before, with local electoral colleges a half-way house on the road to full one-member-one-vote and the end of the trades unions' block vote.[19] Kinnock changed the party's structure, management and methods. An organisation which had, in 1983, drafted the 'longest suicide note in history' became an electoral machine at home with modern communication techniques, from opinion polling through to presentation. He reconnected the party with the young and encouraged it to shuffle off its old-fashioned image.

Nor should it be forgotten that there *were* electoral successes: in the Euro-elections of 1989, in local elections and in by-elections. There were also other successes which, though they did not at first translate into votes, were to prove the more significant in the longer term. Kinnock's political life has been replete with ironies. If it is true, as many analysts have argued, that it was the fear of a Labour victory which led Tory MPs to overthrow Thatcher, then here, perhaps, was Kinnock's biggest success and the greatest irony of all.[20]

Analysis and assessment

Kinnock's political detractors have variously argued that, in an increasingly feverish search for electorability, he betrayed the Labour Party's ideological traditions and its working-class supporters, and that his leadership subsequently turned into a 'personal fiefdom' (Prescott, LWT, 1992). After the 1992 defeat Michael Meacher (who had made a longer journey from the further left during the 1980s and is now a Blairite minister) declared that 'the tragedy is that we lost our sense of soul' (LWT, 1992). Roy Hattersley, more kindly, pointed out the irony of 'the great evangelist politician of this century' presiding over 'the least evangelistic period in the party's history' (idem.) At a more personal level, many argued (including some of his closest friends) that Kinnock, under the influence of his backroom strategists and opinion poll experts, suppressed his own personality in search of electoral respectability, and that in so doing suppressed all that was most attractive about himself. [21]

More academic critiques of Kinnock's leadership tend to one of two converging approaches. The *structuralists* argue that Kinnock was ultimately more interested in the mechanics of power than the underlying principles. They portray his leadership as a series of pragmatic, structure-based moves intended solely to enable the Labour Party to be elected (with the implicit charge that he put personal ambition before ideological commitment). Thus when the 1983–7 organisational and presentational changes failed to deliver, they were followed by the 1987–9 policy review. The structuralists further argue that, to get his way, Kinnock had to resort to procedural tactics and behind-the-scenes, strong-arm tactics rather than open political debate. This increasingly pragmatic search for electorability, especially when combined with an emphasis on the leader's personality, left the party grievously open to charges of opportunism – particularly in 1992.

The *ideologists* argue that the overall review of the Labour Party's policies between 1983 and 1992 was fundamentally flawed because it lacked a coherent theoretical basis. If Kinnock became progressively more convinced about which policies had to be jettisoned, he became progressively less clear about what David Marquand has described as 'a governing philosophy capable of guiding decision-makers through the unforeseeable contingencies of power' (Marquand, 1991, pp. 201–2). The methodology of the policy review, with its *ad hoc* committees and opinion-poll-based logic, seemed to emphasise presentation over philosophy, again laying Kinnock and his party open to the charge of opportunism.

Kinnock has acknowledged elements of truth in both critiques. Having witnessed the professional approach of electorally successful social-democratic parties on the continent (particularly in Scandinavia), he unashamedly laid great emphasis on organisational and presentational change in the 1983–8 period and never relinquished this concern thereafter. In view of the abject experience of Labour's 1983 general election campaign such a change was, for Kinnock, a *sine qua non*.[22] Nevertheless the 'electoralism' of which he was accused was never an end in itself. Presentational and policy changes were part of a continuum designed to update the party and render it relevant again to a broad constituency. In his 1983 speech as the new leader of the party he had quoted Nye Bevan's observation that 'He who would lead must articulate the wants, the frustrations and the aspirations of the majority.' It was a theme to which Kinnock would constantly return.

By his own admission Kinnock was less clear on a new ideological approach and much of his thought and writing in the second half of the 1980s seems, in retrospect, like the search for what he even then called 'the third way'.[23] There are a number of probable explanations for this. A first was that he came to the leadership with a great deal of left-wing ideological commitment which had slowly to be revised. As importantly, and intimately linked to his role as a leader of transition, the political, economic and demographic topography of the ideological battleground was rapidly changing. The end of the Cold War, in particular, led to generalised reflection throughout the Western world about the relative importance of ideology (for example Fukuyama's *The End of History* and the debate it spawned). It is in any case a moot point whether this very lack of a clear-cut alternative ideology enabled him to make the necessary changes. (And it is worth pointing out that the party's leadership today is still searching for a coherent ideological position.)

As to the recurring charges of having put too much emphasis on centralised revisionism, Kinnock has unapologetically argued that 'the complaint should be that there was not enough of either – if centralisation and revision means greater co-ordination and greater ability to conclude and advocate vitally important policies long before an election' (Kinnock, 1994, p. 544). With regard to the charges of a 'cult of personality', it should perhaps be recalled that in both 1987 and 1992 the party's strategy advisers insisted that Kinnock was an electoral asset which should be exploited. In apparent contradiction, a more insidious theory held that by 1992 Kinnock had become an electoral liability and, seeing the writing on the wall, should have resigned in favour of a new leader (almost certainly John Smith) long before the general election. In his own mind Kinnock never faltered in the belief that

> my replacement with anyone else would not have made an improvement, and that no one else could do better. And I wasn't being arrogant in that. I don't think you would have found a combination that was sufficiently determined, willing to go into fine detail, expend the time and detail on endless discussions, and someone who could get up and light the Labour Party's touch paper when the occasion demanded (Jones, 1994, p. 194).

Implicit in this response was Kinnock's determination that the modernisation process which he began in 1983 should be seen through, a view which he subsequently felt had been confirmed by John Smith's more relaxed, 'one-more-heave' attitude towards reform (with the exception of OMOV). By staying in place, Kinnock ensured that his reforms would stick.

The reform process became for Kinnock a very personal mission, which he carried through with almost evangelical fervour. He described his decision to stand for the leadership as 'almost like being called up. What I believed in and wanted to thrive was in peril and I had to do what I had to do to try and defend it' (LWT, 1992).[24] Although the overall leadership experience 'was frequently frustrating, completely unsatisfying', partly because of 'the refusal in some quarters to try and understand what we were about', Kinnock nevertheless believed that he 'had to see it through to the bitter end' (LWT, 1992). Subsequently 'He heaped the blame for Labour's defeat on himself. He felt he had let everyone down: his family, his staff, his party and his country. He had spent nearly a decade trying to make the Labour Party electable and finally came to feel that he was the last obstacle in the way' (Baxter, 1994). He considered himself 'a personal and political failure' (LWT, 1992).

In the context of this study, the question must be posed as to how far Kinnock was a leader of transition and how far he was *led*. Clearly, in introducing change he was responding to a number of important influences. A first was the Thatcherite political agenda and the 're-ordering' of British politics (Kavanagh, 1997, pp. 171–93). International events were a second important group of factors which, if they did not encourage change, at least facilitated it. These included Ronald Reagan's 1979 election, which led both to the siting of Cruise missiles on British soil and to the Star Wars initiative, thus reinforcing CND and unilateralist convictions on the left; François Mitterrand's ill-fated go-it-alone strategy in the 1981–3 period, which did much to undermine the economic philosophy behind Labour's 1983 manifesto and to encourage fiscal consensus among continental social democrats; Mikhail Gorbachev's 1985 appointment, leading to the November 1985 Gorbachev–Reagan Geneva meeting and agreement on mutual arms reductions; and Jacques Delors' 1986–92 internal market initiative.

The proof that Kinnock consciously chose to lead a transition process lies in the fact that other, easier, options were available to him. He could, for example, have opted for more gentle change, hoping in the meantime that support for the Conservative government would naturally decline. It was Kinnock's underlying diagnosis which made such an option untenable for him, and in the end made him victim to a wonderful irony which Roy Hattersley succinctly summarised:

> The convictions which secured him the party leadership, denied him the premiership. For the change opened him to the charge that he had either disguised his beliefs to deceive the voters or abandoned them in order to secure election. In fact, he had done no more than move with the times. And the Labour Party moved with him (Hattersley, 1997, p. 373).

By disqualifying himself in this way, Kinnock had 'made it possible for future Labour leaders to go into 10 Downing Street' (LWT, 1992).[25] As a more critical observer has suggested, 'Kinnock should in the fullness of time be recognised as one of the most successful political leaders in post-war Britain' (McSmith, 1996, p. 17). He had, observed another commentator, 'saved Labour from self-destruction' (Stephens, 1998). That he did so was because, long before he rose to the leadership, Kinnock had grasped Lampedusa's paradoxical truth that 'If we want things to stay as they are, things will have to change.'

Neil Kinnock: chronology

1942, 28 March	Born in Tredegar, a South Wales steel and coal town. His father was a miner, his mother a district nurse.
1955	Joined the Labour Party and became politically active.
1961	Went to University College, Cardiff, to study history and industrial relations. Became chairman of the Socialist Society. Met Glenys Parry.
1965	Elected president of the Cardiff Students' Union. Won pass degree. Began work as a WEA lecturer.
1967, 25 March	Married Glenys and settled in Pontllanfraith, in the Bedwellty Westminster constituency.
1969, 6 June	Selected as Labour prospective parliamentary candidate for the Bedwellty constituency, a massively safe seat.
1970, 18 June	Elected MP with a 23 000 vote majority. Conservative government formed.
1974, 28 February	Reelected MP. Labour government formed.
1975, 1 October	Made name at Tribune rally in the margins of the Labour Party conference.
1978, October	Elected to the NEC.
1979, 3 May	Labour lost general election.

1979, 8 June	Kinnock accepted Front bench position as shadow education spokesman.
1980, November	Callaghan resigned as party leader. Michael Foot elected to replace him.
1981, January	Wembley Party conference created new college for leadership elections.
1981, March	'Gang of Three' quit Labour Party and formed the Social Democratic Party (SDP). Tony Benn challenged Denis Healey for the deputy leadership.
1981, October	Kinnock led group of Tribune Labour MPs in voting for John Silkin in first round and abstaining in the second round. As a consequence Benn's bid was narrowly defeated.
1983, 10 June	Labour suffered a heavy defeat in the general election. Michael Foot subsequently resigned as leader. Kinnock reelected to redrawn Islwyn constituency.
1983, 2 October	Kinnock elected leader with 71.3 per cent of the vote. Roy Hattersley elected deputy leader on 'Dream Ticket'.
1985, October	Conference speech attacking Militant Tendency.
1983–87	Introduced a series of organisational and presentational reforms to the Party. Changed party policies, most notably on EC and council house sales.
1987, 11 June	Labour again defeated in the general election. Kinnock subsequently launched full-scale policy review.
1989, 9 May	Results of policy review published as *Meet the Challenge, Make the Change*.
1989, October	New multilateral defence policy approved by the party conference.
1990–91	Further organisational changes effected to the party.
1990 (early)	Opinion polls gave Labour a 15 per cent lead over the Conservatives. Kinnock overtook Thatcher in voters' estimation of the leader best equipped to be prime minister.
1990, March	Labour won Mid-Staffordshire by-election, overturning a 14 000 Conservative majority.
1990, 22 November	Margaret Thatcher resigned.
1990, 27 November	John Major elected new Conservative leader and prime minister.
1992, 9 April	Labour lost general election. Kinnock subsequently resigned the leadership.
1992, 18 July	John Smith elected leader.
1994, 12 May	John Smith died. Tony Blair elected leader.
1994, December	Kinnock resigned Westminster seat.
1995, January	Kinnock became member of the European Commission.
1997, 1 May	Labour won general Election.

Notes

1 Kinnock did not 'subscribe to the "swing door" view of electoral politics' and, in conjunction, 'he was one of the first to take the SDP threat seri-

ously' (McSmith, 1996, p. 23). Both views stemmed from a belief that the nature of the British electorate was changing.

2   Of the same incident Tony Benn noted that 'he sounded just like a minister' (Benn, 1991, pp. 583–4).

3   This despite his Bedwellty constituency party's overwhelming decision to support Benn.

4   'His socialism is more felt than thought; his politics less from the head, more from the gut' (Rawnsley, 1992, p. 23).

5   'His plan – confided to colleagues in the week of his election – was to draw breath until the New Year and then, after three or four months of personal consolidation, take the dangerous but essential first step back into the mainstream of politics' (Hattersley, 1997, p. 295).

6   Coming, as it did, from a potential leadership candidate, this took some courage. A confidential briefing to Eric Heffer described it as 'a minor political disaster ... whoever wrote the speech should simply be shot' (Kinnock Archives).

7   See Butler and Jowett (1985), pp. 64–5, for an account of the leadership's conversion to the use of polls – despite deeply ingrained suspicion and opposition from 'old-style' Labour politicians.

8   'There were 29 members of the NEC. As the vote started, I was sitting near to Michael Meacher and I said "Michael, if this vote goes the wrong way you can say goodbye to any prospect of a Labour government." And he said, "You really mean that, don't you?" And I said to him "I know it"' (Kinnock on LWT). Kinnock subsequently lost the 1985 Conference vote, but he had won his NEC majority (see McSmith, 1996, pp. 50–51).

9   One commentator has pointed out that Kinnock expanded the size of his front bench team – thereby also extending the leader's patronage (McSmith, 1996, p. 20).

10   'Where others of seemingly greater stature – Clement Attlee, Hugh Gaitskell, Harold Wilson, Jim Callaghan, Michael Foot or John Smith – looked down in bewilderment at the strange tribes who made up the Labour Party, Kinnock understood and was directly engaged with them' (McSmith, 1996, p. 17) As Kinnock has put it, this insider status meant that he could say to others 'It doesn't hurt. Take it from me, changing isn't betrayal of what we believe in. It is the only proper way to *uphold* what we believe in.' (Interview with the author, 23 December 1998).

11   See Butler and Butler (1994), p. 237 for detailed statistics.

12   Kinnock himself saw this as a crucial point 'It refutes the claim that the SDP was a catalyst for change. On the contrary, its existence *slowed* change' (interview with the author, 23 December 1998).

13   'Neil understood better than most the sociological processes involved. He saw this through his own children' (Merlyn Rees interview). As Morgan has pointed out, Kinnock came from 'a new South Wales, an updated, upwardly mobile, welfarized society, the product of the Labour revolution after 1945' (Morgan, 1997, p. 335).

14   'they developed a crucially important function as progress chasers and troubleshooters and – formally and informally – I was able to secure direct involvement in all policy groups and decisions without seeming to sit on anyone's shoulder' (Kinnock, 1994, p. 544).

15 If Prescott had defeated Hattersley, Kinnock would have resigned (Kinnock on LWT, 1992).

16 Gould went on to argue that 'three images of the party were dominant in the 1983 General Election: division, extremism and weakness (Gould, 1998, p. 20). Kinnock extirpated them all.

17 'By 1983–4 it was widely predicted that the party ... was about to undergo the same kind of "strange death" that the Liberal Party had suffered sixty years earlier' (Morgan, 1997, p. 723).

18 23 December 1998 interview with the author.

19 'He was the one who had spent years prevailing upon the unions that they would have to let go of some of their powers if the Labour Party was to be made electable. He had set the pace, and would have completed the task if circumstances had not required him to give up the job of managing the party' (McSmith, 1996, p. 29).

20 'But Kinnock was a victim of his own success. The Tories began to think his image-builders had made him electable. Even the growing Gulf crisis failed to turn to the Tories' advantage. The unprecedented poll leads for Labour through the summer of 1990 became too good. They led directly to the loss of one of Kinnock's greatest assets, Thatcher' (McKie, 1992, p. 29).

21 'The greatest mistake, however, is that Neil's advisers would not allow him to be himself' (Castle, 1993, p. 583). Kinnock himself dismisses the argument as 'sentimentalist': 'The sort of relaxation these people had in mind would have brought crucifixion by a press pack looking for any evidence of the "firebrand" Kinnock' (interview with the author, 23 December 1998).

22 Nor should it be forgotten that, at the time of his election to the leadership, Kinnock was being urged to engage urgently in precisely such structural change. A 7 October 1983 *New Statesman* editorial, for example, argued that his first priority should be 'the reorganisation of the various elements of the Labour Party machine. In the formulation and presentation of policy the Labour Party has for a considerable time been a shambles.'

23 'A third way is needed; separate and distinct from the stale vanguardism of the ultra-left and from the atavistic and timid premise of social democracy. And that third way has always existed – it is the socialism which, in Aneurin Bevan's definition, "is based on the conviction that free people can use free institutions to *solve* the social and economic problems of the day"' (Kinnock, 1986b, p. 1).

24 'I was responsible for the policy and I will live with it or die with it. As it happened, I died' (Kinnock, 1994, p. 554).

25 At the 1992 Labour Party Conference (that is, long before he became leader), Tony Blair described how Kinnock had created the image 'by a lot of personal courage and a sense of vision about what a modern Labour Party should look like that will be an inspiration to me and many others like me for the rest of our political lives' (LWT, 1992).

References

Baxter, Sarah (1994) 'Mr and Mrs Europe', *Sunday Times*, 25 September, pp. 19–26.

BBC (1998) 'Grammar School Boy' (Timewatch).

Benn, Tony (1991) *Conflicts of Interest* (London: Arrow).

Butler, David, and Gareth Butler (1994) *British Political Facts 1900–1994* (London: Macmillan).

Butler, David, and Paul Jowett (1985) *Party Strategies in Britain* (London: Macmillan).

Butler, David, and Dennis Kavanagh (1984) *The British General Election of 1983* (London: Macmillan).

Castle, Barbara (1993) *Fighting all the Way* (London: Macmillan).

Drower, George M. F. (1984) *Neil Kinnock: The Path to Leadership* (London: Weidenfeld and Nicolson).

Drower, George M. F. (1994) *Kinnock* (Essex: The Publishing Corporation).

Fukuyama, Francis (1992) T*he End of History and the Last Man* (London: Hamilton).

Gould, Philip (1998) *The Unfinished Revolution* (London: Little, Brown).

Harris, Robert (1984) *The Making of Neil Kinnock* (London: Faber and Faber).

Hattersley, Roy (1997) *Fifty Years On* (London: Little, Brown).

Hughes, Colin, and Patrick Wintour (1990) *Labour Rebuilt* (London: Fourth Estate).

Jones, Eileen (1994) *Neil Kinnock* (London: Robert Hale Ltd).

Jones, Tudor (1996) *Remaking the Labour Party* (London: Routledge).

Judge, David (1993) *The Parliamentary State* (London: Sage).

Kavanagh, Dennis (1997) *The Reordering of British Politics* (Oxford: Oxford University Press).

King, Anthony (ed.) (1992) *Britain at the Polls 1992* (London: Chatham House).

Kinnock Archives, Churchill College, Cambridge.

Kinnock, Neil (1983a) speech to the Socialist Group in the European Parliament (author's archive).

Kinnock, Neil (1983b) 'My Socialism', *New Statesman*, vol. 106, no. 2742 (7 October).

Kinnock, Neil (1986a) *Making Our Way* (Oxford: Basil Blackwell).

Kinnock, Neil (1986b) *The Future of Socialism*, Fabian Tract no. 509 (London).

Kinnock, Neil (1992) *Thorns and Roses, Speeches 1983–1991* (Introduction by Peter Kellner) (London: Hutchinson).

Kinnock, Neil (1994) 'Reforming the Labour Party', *Contemporary Record*, vol. 8, no. 3 (Winter).

Lampedusa, Giuseppe Tomassi di (1987) *The Leopard (Il Gattopardo)* (London: Collins Harvill).

Leapman, Michael (1987) *Kinnock* (London: Unwin).

LWT (London Weekend Television) (1992) 'Kinnock: The Inside Story'.

Marquand, David (1991) *The Progressive Dilemma: From Lloyd George to Kinnock* (London: Heinemann).

McKibbin, Ross (1997) 'Why the Tories Lost', *London Review of Books*, 3 July.

McKie, David (ed.) (1992) *The Election: A Voter's Guide* (London: Fourth Estate).

McSmith, Andy (1996) *Faces of Labour* (London: Verso).

Morgan, Kenneth O. (1997) *Callaghan: A Life* (Oxford: Oxford University Press).

Mortimer, John (1986) *Character Parts* (London: Viking).

Owen, David (1991). *Time to Declare* (London: Michael Joseph).

Pimlott, Ben (1995) *Frustrate Their Knavish Tricks* (London: HarperCollins).

Rawnsley, Andrew (1992) 'Last chance for the Larynx of Fire', in David McKie (ed.), *The Election: A Voter's Guide* (London: Fourth Estate).
Richards, Steve (1998) 'Interview: Neil Kinnock', *New Statesman*, 2 January.
Sopel, John (1995) *Tony Blair* (London: Little, Brown).
Stark, Leonard P. (1996) *Choosing a Leader* (London: Macmillan).
Stephens, Philip (1998) 'New Image for the New Left', *Financial Times*, 31 October–1 November.
Westlake, Martin (1999) 'Neil Kinnock, 1983–1992', in Kevin Jefferys (ed.), *Labour Leaders* (London: I.B. Tauris).
Wintour, Patrick (1992) 'Labour's Search for a Lasting Unity', in David McKie (ed.), *The Election, A Voter's Guide* (London: Fourth Estate).

Interviews

Carl Batten, 11 April 1998 (Tredegar contemporary).
James Callaghan, 6 March 1997.
Barbara Castle, 21 January 1997.
Denis Healey, 22 January 1997.
Merlyn Rees, 31 July 1998.

Adolfo Suárez

Great speed was required to achieve change in order to prevent the rein-
forcement of resistance and to avoid the terrible risk of forgetting the past
(Adolfo Suárez, 1995, p. 51)

Adolfo Suárez, outgoing Prime Minister, runs down the stairs of the Cortes to
help Deputy Prime Minister Gutiérrez Mellado during the abortive 1981 *coup*
attempt. (*Copyright © Agencia EFE*)

6
Adolfo Suárez: Democratic Dark Horse

Simon Parlier

> *Great speed was required to achieve change in order to prevent the reinforcement of resistance and to avoid the terrible risk of forgetting the past* (Adolfo Suárez, 1995, p. 51)

Forgotten by history, ignored in favour of other Spanish politicians such as Felipe González and, above all, the 'democratic king', Juan Carlos, Adolfo Suárez and the role he played in the democratisation of Spain were recognised late, more than ten years after his resignation in 1981. Yet he was the key figure in the Spanish transition process, the lynchpin around whom the whole process was to unfold. Suárez forced the pace with great political dexterity and demonstrated considerable personal courage in his determined quest for the democratisation of Spain. In the context of this study, a fundamental question must be posed. Was Suárez carried by the surge of uncontrollable events once he came to power or did he, of his own will and after due deliberation, accelerate the course of history? Was he, in other words, a true leader of transition? The speed of the transition process, the reasoning and the strategy behind the measures he took, all with the specific aim of ending the authoritarian Francoist regime (notwithstanding the physical risks involved), together with the final political sacrifice; these facts all militate in favour of the conclusion that Suárez was a determined leader of transition.

The political context

In 1976 Adolfo Suárez was singled out by King Juan Carlos to succeed Carlos Arias Navarro as prime minister. Navarro had himself succeeded Admiral Carrero Blanco, Franco's personally chosen dauphin, who was assassinated by an ETA commando on 20 December 1973. With the death of Carrero died also the possibility of continuing with a similar authoritarian regime after Franco's death. The subsequent appointment of the Arias Navarro government already raised the possibility of some liberalisation, but the continued reticence and resistance of the political class decided the king in favour of accelerating the transition process.

The change had, in effect, been initiated in the early 1970s with the rise to power of a new technocratic elite in Francoist Spain, mostly drawn from the Opus Dei stable. But by the mid 1970s those same technocratic elites – promoted by the *Caudillo* in an effort to get Spain out of its international isolation, and with their power based on the economic development of the country – were no longer in control of the process which they had themselves encouraged: the modernisation of a country which had been consigned to the margins of Western Europe since the civil war in the 1930s. A society of mass consumption had been established, the process of secularisation continued apace, the traditional authorities – the army, the family, the Catholic church – were all beginning to be contested and, following the oil crisis of 1973, the economic situation was beginning to deteriorate. What is frequently referred to as the Francoist 'bunker' tended to isolate itself more and more from the society it had awoken. The signs of the new political and economic maturity were muted, but they were there: rebellion in the universities, strikes, regionalist and independence movements, and the thunderclap which ETA's assassination of Admiral Carrero in the centre of Madrid represented. To crown it all, the pillars of the regime itself began to crack and crumble. Reformist currents stirred in the Church and even in the army, whilst the Phalangists, marginalised by the general himself, lost increasing amounts of ground. Into this context was born the deaf struggle between liberals and conservatives, between those who favoured breaking with Francoism and those who wished to carry on, whilst the health of the head of state himself became increasingly uncertain. Moreover, on the international scene, Spain, which had tried to come out from its isolation, had once again been ostracised following the condemnation and execution of three ETA militants at the end of the second Burgos process in September 1975. This isolation was even more disquieting given that Spain's neighbour, Portugal, had experienced its 'revolution of flowers' the previous year.

Finally acknowledged by Franco as his successor, Juan Carlos became king of Spain on 27 November 1975, one week after the death of the *Caudillo*. It is important to remember that until 1977 Spanish politics was run entirely by appointees. The Arias Navarro government, initially reticent, soon revealed itself to be deeply conservative. Juan Carlos decided to force the pace, but with patience. Thus Adolfo Suárez was appointed leader of the Spanish government on 3 July 1976, with the approval of only a part of the Royal Council but the king's firm support. Suárez had first entered government the previous year, when he was appointed as minister for the *Movimiento* (the former Phalangist National Movement) in the Arias Navarro government. A 'young wolf', just 43 years old, Adolfo Suárez was suspected by the opposition of being a late offshoot of the old Francoism: ambitious and intelligent, certainly, but firmly from the *Seraglio*.

Suárez enjoyed both political and personal support from the king. He was, for example, one of the few Spanish politicians who could address Juan Carlos using the more familiar *tu* form. The relationship had formed during Suárez's years as governor of Segovia and then as director general of Spanish television, but also during his time in the Arias government when, as minister for the *Movimiento*, Suárez had successfully defended a draft law on associations which represented a first, timid step towards a more open regime. Suárez had qualities which the opposition, as much as the Francoist elite, could appreciate: a practising Catholic, linked to Francoism, he was also young and seemed open to modernisation. But the support of the king was essential to their joint reformist project. As commander in chief of the armed forces, Juan Carlos represented the first defence against any attempted *coups d'état*, a permanent menace which was one of the primary worries of Spain's first democratic government since 1936.[1]

The Suárez–Juan Carlos relationship was profoundly symbiotic. Juan Carlos was determined to see a fully democratic, constitutional, parliamentary monarchy established in Spain. But this aim meant that he had to maintain a discrete, back-room role. He could proffer advice and gently make his views known, but he could not – and could not be seen to – interfere in the due political process of Spain's embryonic democracy. Hence it fell to his preferred prime minister, Suárez, to make the shared vision a reality, and it was thus Suárez who led the transition process from the front.

Suárez in the transition process

Spain's transition from dictatorship to democracy was both a historical exception and a model in the Western world. It was an exception because the particularity of Spain – unification imposed on a pluri-national country by civil war, then by the Francoist state – meant that the regional question had to be settled at the same time as the transition to democracy. But it was also a model because of the logical and highly intelligent way in which the process was encouraged to unfold. In effect, each step in the transition process dovetailed with and was dependent on its predecessors. Two broad phases were involved. The first ran from Suárez's 1975 appointment to the Arias government through to the formation of the first UDC (Union of the Democratic Centre) government in 1977. The second began with the 1978 establishment of the new parliamentary monarchy and ended with Suárez's resignation as prime minister in 1981.[2]

The 'suicide' of the Francoist Cortes

The first Suárez government, established in July 1976, was a transitional body made up of appointed members representing various elements of the post-Franco state (political parties were not yet recognised), many of them hostile to the sort of reform the king and his new prime minister wanted to introduce. Yet the first major task facing the new government was also the most difficult, for the intrinsically Francoist houses of the *Cortes* had to be converted to the principle of universal suffrage – which in effect, would be tantamount to suicide for the old-style coopted members, or *procuradores*. The fact that Suárez, aided and abetted by strategically-placed sympathisers of the reform programme, was able to achieve such a result was an early indication of his sophisticated political skills.

The government's reformist programme (in reality that of Juan Carlos and Suárez) envisaged a number of vital, interlinked planks, including the legalisation of political parties, a general amnesty for political crimes, laws enshrining democratic rights and freedoms, the return of the exiles of 1939 and, last but not least, the organisation of free elections. The opposition had been given an initial indication of the sincerity of the government's reformist intentions when, notwithstanding the hostility of one of the two deputy prime ministers, a first, limited political amnesty was granted by royal decree. But the amnesty was only possible because the king's initiative had been taken without prior consultation of the Royal Council, a fiercely conservative body which would normally be consulted on constitutional issues and would surely have blocked such a move.

Some reformists argued that, since Francoist blocking majorities were built into the existing constitutional arrangements, the only way of realising the government's plans for political reform would be to bypass the Cortes, and for the reforms to be legitimised directly through a popular referendum and then presented to the Cortes as a *fait accompli*. But Suárez realised that on the more fundamental issue of suffrage he could not challenge the general legality of the existing constitutional order; the new had to be legitimised by the old. It was therefore decided that the political reform law would have to be adopted by the old Francoist *Cortes* before being put to the people.[3]

Thus it was the *procuradores* themselves, meeting in plenary session, who signed their own death warrant in November 1976. To get this remarkable result Suárez relied heavily on the support of the president of the Cortes, Torcuato Fernández Miranda, who facilitated the passage of the bill with great skill. To shorten the debates, a sort of guillotine procedure was imposed, and the various *rapporteurs* on the law were selected judiciously. The carefully-honed arguments they advanced stressed the futility of opposition and the economic and political advantages of modernisation. The resulting vote was crushing: of the 497 *procuradores* present, 425 approved the reform, 59 voted against it and 13 abstained. So it was that Francoism was beaten; on its own territory, in its own institutions and by its own representatives. Suárez rightly saw this vote as being vital to the democratisation process, since it legitimised the transition and acted as a trigger for a second round of reforms.

In the ensuing popular referendum, 94 per cent of those voting approved the reform, and more than 77 per cent of the electorate turned out to vote, even though the Communist Party, the Socialist Parties (the PSOE and the Social Democratic Federation), the Catalonian Assembly, the Basque Nationalist Party (PNV) and the Galician independents had all called on their supporters to abstain. Not only did this massive approval strengthen the government's reformist hand *vis-à-vis* the more conservative Francoist elements in the government's own ranks, but it also forced the left-wing opposition and the regionalist parties to clarify their own positions and lend more open support to the government and its programme. The gamble – for nobody could have foreseen such a crushing result – had paid off handsomely.

Reforming without purging: the neutralisation of the army

Although there were a few liberal and reformist officers in the Spanish army, and although the army was ready to accept some relaxation of the political system, the majority of its members remained intimately linked to the Francoist regime and therefore closely monitored the transition process. The army was instinctively loyal to the monarchy, and opinions varied among the different regiments and forces, but the implicit menace of a *putsch* was ever-present throughout Suárez's stewardship of the reform process.[4] Once the succession to Franco had been successfully managed within the old state framework, the immediate threat of a *coup* receded a little but, as countless rumours constantly revealed, the possibility remained. Repeated efforts to destabilise the regime were made by both the extreme right and the extreme left. A military plot was uncovered in November 1978, and there was the abortive 1981 attempt led by Lieutenant-Colonel Tejero and General Jaime Milans del Bosch.

Suárez was well aware of the menace, and he knew that he had at all costs to avoid the sort of outright confrontation which might tip the armed forces into the reactionary camp. (The tension between military and civil authorities was apparent from the day the Suárez government entered office.) At the same time he could not leave an inherently conservative general staff the sort of room for manoeuvre which might enable it to block the transition process.

The older and more superior ranks of the army remained scarred by their experiences in the Spanish Civil War and had difficulty recognising those they had opposed in 1939 as legitimate political actors, let alone witnessing their return to power; this applied particularly to the Communist Party, whose legalisation, they knew, was on the not-too-distant agenda. Nor could they accept any questioning of the unity of the Spanish state, though the plurality of Spain had been recognised and decentralisation and devolution were, after the reintegration of the Communist Party, the avowed second priority of the new government.

As the government was being formed, Juan Carlos shrewdly advised Suárez to leave in place those military ministers who had shown little enthusiasm for the reform process in the previous administration, in the hope that their presence in the government would compromise the views they represented.

The first friction between Suárez and the army occurred in relation to the August 1976 amnesty, but open military opposition became apparent when the government began to draft a law concerning trades union rights. This open hostility, relayed and amplified by the more reactionary parts of the press (such as the newspaper, *Alcazar*) was only finally overcome when the focal point for the opposition, General de Santiago, was replaced by the more liberal Lieutenant-General Gutiérrez Mellado in the sensitive post of deputy prime minister for military affairs (military ministers would later be grouped together within the Ministry of Defence).

In addition to the appointment of reliable allies and the gradual creation of a network of support to keep the military on board, Suárez also skilfully exploited the tactic of the *fait accompli*. Thus he assured the army that it was impossible to envisage the legalisation of the Communist Party until it abandoned its revolutionary programme, but he did not specify that the party would be recognised if this condition were satisfied. He denied having deceived the army on this issue and when his political legitimacy was questioned by the more stubborn militarists he did not hesitate to face them down. Thus when the outgoing General de Santiago insidiously hinted at the threat of a *coup d'état*, Suárez brutally reprimanded him by pointing out that 'the death penalty remains in force in Spain'. To reassure and to consult, to remain firm on the pre-eminence of the civil authorities but to rely on the support of the more sympathetic parts of the army; in this way Suárez managed – notwithstanding the legalisation of the Communist Party, the establishment of regional autonomy and above all ETA terrorism – to avoid a military rebellion until 23 February 1981.

Consolidating the monarchy and dividing the opposition: the legalisation of the Communist Party

Winning the participation in the transition process of the left-wing opposition parties was no less of a challenge to Suárez. The prime minister had to rally them around whilst convincing them to abandon both their republicanism and their revolutionary ideology. Paradoxically it was not the more moderate PSOE (even if, notwithstanding the efforts of Felipe González, the party was reluctant to abandon its Marxist terms of reference) which became the government's privileged interlocutor but the Communist Party, despite the fact that the latter enjoyed less potential electoral support. The paradox was partly explained by the fact that Santiago Carrillo's Communist Party remained influential in Spanish society, notably through workers' committees. Above all, in symbolic terms the legalisation of the Communist Party would signify the true end of the civil war. In tactical terms, if Suárez could win the support of Carrillo (who was forbidden to live on Spanish territory but had re-entered the country clandestinely), this would oblige the PSOE to clarify its own position and thus divide the opposition. This in turn would facilitate a victory for the centre, which was Suárez's underlying ambition.

Initial hesitation over whether to legalise the Communist Party before or after the promised elections was rapidly overcome – in effect, to have legalised the party afterwards would have robbed the democratisation process of its credibility. Therefore in order truly to consolidate the transition process, it was imperative that, after the legalisation of the other political parties (February 1977) and the re-establishment of the right to strike (March 1977), the communists should be reintegrated into Spanish political life. Following secret negotiations and the release of Santiago Carrillo (who had been arrested in December 1976 and provisionally held in detention), the first meeting between the two men took place on 27 February 1977.

The communist secretary general held some strong cards in his hand and did not hesitate to use them. He knew that without him the transition process, which he had watched closely from the beginning, could not be complete. At the same time he was aware of the strong determination of the prime minister and had been quick to see that his first impressions of Suárez as a Francoist offshoot, which he had shared with so many others, were wrong. Embarked with its French and Italian *confrères* on the movement dubbed 'Eurocommunism', the Spanish Communist Party had taken its distance from Moscow and was sincere in its desire to play a part in the democratisation process. To recognise the monarchy, the flag and the unity of Spain and to abandon references to a socialist state; these were the sacrifices required of Santiago Carrillo.

At this stage in the transition process, and without being certain of the communists' sincerity, Adolfo Suárez decided to make the first move and legalised the PCE, having taken the precaution of ensuring that the decision was accepted by the competent authorities. Subsequently, on 9 April 1977 the Junta de Fiscales declared that there were no facts to incriminate the party for illegal association in accordance with Article 172 of the Penal Code. 'The war is finished!' declared a friend of Carrillo (Abella, 1997, p. 173). Once the more virulent reactions of the extreme conservatives in the military and governing classes had passed, the Communist Party accepted almost all of the conditions which Suárez had imposed. From then on

Santiago Carrillo became one of the government's most loyal and reliable allies. Once again, Suárez had successfully taken a shrewd gamble.

Winning in the centre to avoid polarisation: the first legislative elections

In 1977, in the middle of the democratic transition process, Spain's first general elections since 1936 took place. With considerable difficulty Suárez managed to create a Union of the Democratic Centre (UCD), as the opinion polls had convinced him that he had to unite together in a centrist bloc the reformists, the Christian democrats and the social democrats. Contrary to the tactics chosen by Manuel Fraga Iribarne, who had rebuffed Suárez's centrist approaches and hoped, through the creation of his Popular Alliance (AP), to construct a moderate-conservative bloc on the right, Suárez wanted to avoid a left–right confrontation, afraid that this might resurrect the spectre of the civil war.

Suárez's approach was vindicated. At the end of a campaign notable for the extensive use of radio and television, and thanks to a partly proportional electoral system weighted in favour of the rural provinces, the UCD beat the PSOE, winning 34.71 per cent votes and 165 seats against 29.24 per cent and 118 seats. The win was relative but the result was vitally significant in one important respect: with the poor showing of the AP on the right (8.39 per cent of the votes and 16 seats) and the mediocre performance by the PCE on the left (9.24 per cent of the votes and 20 seats), the result had been simultaneously anti-Francoist and anticommunist. The polarisation Suárez had feared had thus been avoided and Spain's new democracy could now become 'routine'.

The UCD, which would probably never have existed without Suárez's determination, was never more than an electoral cartel, and its inherent contradictions would soon have their effect on the political destiny of the prime minister. Nevertheless, at that particular stage in the democratisation process Suárez's instincts had clearly been right. Moreover, the achievement of a relative majority, even if the result for the liberals had been disappointing, also helped to encourage and rally the other most important actors in the transition.

Putting an end to Francoist centralism whilst assuring national unity: regional autonomy

The recognition of the pluralist nature of the Spanish nation was an essential element in the democratisation process. The Generalitat of Catalonia had been abolished in 1938 soon after its recreation by the republicans. Its former president, Josep Tarradellas, was still in exile in France and the Catalonian nationalists were becoming increasingly impatient. But the situation was far worse in the Basque region, where ETA had opted for a military strategy, although its clear attempts to destabilise the transition process were unsuccessful.

Thus it was decided that devolution would first take place in Catalonia. The aim was to grant the rebel province a large degree of autonomy whilst avoiding any unilateral and illegal re-establishment of the Generalitat and making sure that the integral nature of the Spanish nation was not menaced. The negotiations were preceded by a number of gestures demonstrating the government's good faith; for example, when Suárez visited Barcelona the day after the referendum on the political reform package – which was approved by 94.2 per cent of the voters in Catalonia – he announced the re-establishment of Catalan as an official language on a par with Castillian and the imminent drafting of a statute of independence, with the work to be undertaken by a council composed of future Catalan deputies and senators.

But in his opening position, Tarradellas set himself against direct negotiations between the Catalonians and the government, was opposed to the 'half measures' proposed and demanded that he should be allowed to return as president of the Generalitat. For his part, Suárez was ready to accept the symbolically important legitimacy of the old Catalonian leader but only on condition that Tarradellas recognised the Spanish monarchy and the unity of Spain, and that he participated in the overall administrative decentralisation process. The simple re-establishment of the Generalitat was thus excluded from the very beginning, and in July 1977 the tough, frank discussions between Suárez and Tarradellas finally resulted in a compromise. The government undertook to re-establish the Catalonian institutions but without specifying a timetable and without defining what form this future self-administration would take. Instead a transitional formula was agreed. The old 1932 statute would not be mentioned and the definitive arrangement would be decided by the Cortes. Tarradellas would not be recognised as president of the Generalitat but would be accorded the title of 'Honourable'. On 11 September 1977 the Catalonian people were able to celebrate their national feast day for the first time since 1939 and new negotiations, between government representatives and Tarradellas but also this time with the Catalonian political parties, got under way, ultimately leading to the Perpignan agreement, signed on 28 September 1977. It was a 'spectacular political coup' (Preston, 1986, p. 132).

Under the agreement the Generalitat would be re-established on the basis of three general principles: the unity of Spain and solidarity among all its component peoples; recognition of Catalonia, as symbolised by the provisional Generalitat; and the Generalitat to be reconstituted and developed in conformity with the law and without setting any conditions for the future draft constitution. The Catalonian question was therefore settled within the current constitutional framework by decree and not by any sudden rupture from the past, with all of the consequences that this would necessarily have entailed. Suárez knew that he could not grant full autonomy to any one province because it would inevitably encourage the other provinces to make similar claims. It was for this reason that the government refused to countenance the reintroduction of the *fueros* (the old autonomous institutions) in the Basque region, since this would necessarily have entailed the recognition of a form of sovereignty distinct from that of the Spanish people. It was because of the government's intransigence on this issue that the Basque nationalists abstained in large numbers in the later referendum on the Spanish constitution.

The three provinces were thus granted provisional autonomous status by royal decree, with the government and the moderate nationalists of the Basque National Party (PNV) managing to reach agreement in July 1979. In effect Suárez sought to dilute Basque and Catalonian nationalism in an overall context of decentralisation. This was done by recognising the existence of nationalities – but not of nations, and through the simultaneous establishment of a series of 'preautonomous' arrangements in Galicia, Valencia, the Canary Islands, Andalusia, Extramaduras, Castille-Leon and the Balearic Islands.

Governing with the tacit support of the opposition: the Moncloa pact

Whilst the first Suárez government (1976–77) was occupied with the initial steps in the transition process, the economic and social situation in the country continued to worsen. The 1973 oil crisis had led to a worrying deficit in the balance of payments, the inflation rate stood at 42 per cent, and Spain's foreign debt amounted to some 12 billion dollars. The second Suárez government (1977–81) was therefore forced to turn its attention to the economy, recognising that the democratisation process would be threatened by any further decline in the social climate and that some sort of political compromise would thus be necessary. Suárez had a choice: once he had presented his proposal on the economy to the Council of Ministers he could take it to the Cortes where, as a minority government, he could count on the support of the nationalist parties, or he could try to seek much broader approval.

With characteristic lucidity, he opted for the second course. He saw that broad political support, and particularly the support of the opposition left, would enable the government to attack the economic crisis far more effectively. Moreover, communist support for the government would put pressure on the socialists to give their full support not only to his consensual policy on the economy but also to constitutional reform, which would be the decisive step in the transition to full democracy. Thus, whilst the deputy prime minister for economic affairs was putting together a crisis package, the representatives of all of the trades unions were convoked in order to convince them of the seriousness of the situation and hence to be moderate in their salary claims. The aim was to reach agreement on a 'social pact' which as a *quid pro quo* would also include a draft workers' statute (borrowing from the 1969 Italian experiment), an initiative the workers' councils were sure to welcome.

Hence the Moncloa Pact, as it was dubbed, was at one and the same time economic (reducing the public debt, supporting the peseta), social (fiscal reforms, the workers' statute) and political (freedom of expression, reorganisation of the forces of order, amendments to the code of military justice, de-penalising adultery, living together outside marriage and contraception). It was duly accepted by the trades unions and signed by most of the political parties on 25 October 1977. On the opposition left, Santiago Carrillo's unreserved support (which he had previously signalled to Suárez) was a crucial determining factor. Thus, an earlier reformist measure, the legalisation of the Communist Party, had now borne fruit. The 'historic compromise', which the economic and political right opposed in vain, not only enabled Suárez to show the Spanish people that he had kept his word, but also to correct the economic situation. The inflation rate fell from

26.4 per cent at the end of 1977 to 16 per cent in 1978. The balance of payments deficit was cut by half. Foreign currency reserves swelled, and companies' share prices increased. But the principal effects of the Moncloa Pact were undoubtedly political, as yet more obstacles on the way to full democratisation were cleared away. The threat of social unrest, perhaps not as dangerous as separatism but still a potential obstacle, had been overcome.

Ratification of the transition: the approval of the constitution

Adolfo Suárez was strongly aware of the traps into which the Second Spanish Republic had fallen and which had brought about its downfall. His characteristically consensual aim therefore was not a constitutional arrangement decided by one half of the country and imposed on the other half, but rather a new constitution elaborated by all of the political forces in the country and ratified by the newly elected Cortes, acting as a sort of constituent assembly.

A number of fundamental disputes had to be overcome before such a constitution could be drafted. Among these were the very nature of the envisaged state, the separation of the Church and the state, the regional question, and public rights and freedoms. It was this last topic which first provoked conflict and menaced the *politica de la concordia* when an amendment relating to the suspension of fundamental rights in exceptional circumstances (a measure designed to help in the struggle against terrorism) provoked strong protests, particularly among the socialists, who at that stage had still not abandoned their republicanism. At the last moment the socialists abandoned their insistence on the inclusion of the term 'Republic' in return for the abolition of the death penalty and the lowering of the age of majority to 18, thus enabling Article 1.3 of the draft constitution to define Spain as a parliamentary monarchy.

The regional question also provoked lively and passionate debate. The compromise solution ultimately chosen recognised Spanish 'nationalities', but not 'nations' or 'peoples'. With regard to the Church and the state there were equally fierce debates, ranging from those who argued for recognition of the Church's role in Spanish society to the historical anticlericalism of the left. But here too a compromise was reached, with a secular state and freedom of education.

This intense phase of passionate discussion enabled all of the different political actors involved to exchange their points of view directly and to look beyond the traditional political cleavages, facilitating understanding and political compromise. The resulting draft constitution was adopted almost unanimously by the two chambers of the Cortes and ratified by 87.7 per cent of the electorate. Only in the Basque region, where the Basque National Party called for its supporters to abstain (50 per cent did so), was this resounding success diminished.

Legitimising and entrenching the democratic transition: the second legislative elections

The 1979 announcement of new legislative elections and the holding of municipal elections coincided with an increase in ETA terrorist activities and, as a consequence, rumours of an imminent *coup d'état*. By announcing the elections Suárez hoped to capitalise on his previous successes and perhaps win an absolute majority. But already the tone of the political debate had changed.

Felipe González tried to turn the election campaign into a struggle between the camouflaged right and an honest and moderate socialist left. Worried by opinion poll predictions, Suárez adopted the opposite strategy. He pointed to his government's achievements to date and announced his future reformist agenda. These could only be undermined by the terrorist threat, he argued, implicitly raising fears of Marxist agitation. He accused González's PSOE of ambiguity and – because of its unreasonable insistence on pet socialist projects such as liberalisation, abortion, nationalisation and self-management – of undue radicalism. The underlying theme was that the Socialist Party had not yet achieved political maturity, despite the reformist will of its leader. Suárez also played up the divisions between the opposition parties, since the socialists effectively refused to countenance any sort of united strategy on the left with the communists.

Following on from the successful tactics of the *politica de la concordia*, the new strategy of confrontation proved similarly effective, with the UCD winning 35.2 per cent of the vote as against 32.3 per cent for the PSOE. The strategy was not entirely successful for the prime minister as his government remained a minority one and was dependent on the support of the Allianza Popular.[5] The elections nevertheless represented an important occasion for testing the strength of the transition process since, for the first time, the political forces participated in genuine and open political confrontation. Thus Spanish democracy began to take root.

Sacrificing power rather than endangering the democratisation process: Suárez's resignation

I had governed for almost five years with a minority. To continue in this way would have been very complicated. Then a censure motion was tabled and although I won it technically I lost it morally. In turn, I tabled a confidence motion which I also won, but neither win enabled me to overcome the erosion to which my political authority had been subjected (Suárez, 1996, p. 247).

Adolfo Suárez's resignation has been interpreted in a number of ways, some even suggesting that he was afraid he would otherwise be deposed by a military *coup d'état*. But it seems that, on the contrary, although he knew that part of the army was hostile towards him and even, through the intelligence of the Ministry of Defence, was aware of the different possible scenarios for a *coup de force*, Suárez decided to resign in order to protect and consolidate the emerging democracy which he considered largely to have been his creation.

Since the elections of 1979 the political situation had deteriorated considerably. The ETA terrorist campaign had intensified. The PSOE had launched a parliamentary offensive by tabling a censure motion. Suárez's own political camp was disintegrating, with a part of it seeking *rapprochement* with Manuel Fraga's party on the right. Suárez had fallen out with his deputy prime minister, Fernando Abril, and there were rumours in the press about a 'Gaullian' solution. All political parties, including the PSOE, began bargaining in view of the possible formation of a government of national unity or of 'public health'. It was in this context that Suárez, who also sensed that he no longer had the unambiguous support of the king, decided to resign.

Suárez's principal failure, one which he himself acknowledged, was his inability to form a genuine party. Even if he had managed to merge the component elements of the UCD, the 'barons' retained their positions and after the 1979 elections Suárez's leadership was increasingly questioned. The erosion was exacerbated by the advances made by the left in the municipal elections, the electoral setbacks in Catalonia, in the Basque region and Andalusia (during the February 1980 referendum on autonomy). At the same time Suárez never saw the creation of a genuine political party as a priority, seeing his essential task rather as one of avoiding confrontation between the left and the right. Moreover, it is questionable whether it would have been possible to create a party, given the speed of the transition process and the short period of time available to him. As to the risk of a *putsch*, the great irony is that, instead of diminishing the risk through his resignation, Suárez may actually have partly and indirectly encouraged it by creating a political vacuum which the conspirators then sought to fill. Nor was the voluntary sacrifice of Suárez – the man who, together with the king, had been one of the principal initiators and architects of Spanish democracy – recompensed in the 1982 elections (nor, incidentally, was Santiago Carrillo rewarded as he might have been). Commentators saw in this fact the justification for the outgoing prime minister's strategy, since the Spanish did not see fit to reward Suárez for his sacrifice but turned resolutely to the future; 'this popular ingratitude demonstrated the excellence of the post-1975 strategy' (Hermet, 1986, p. 290).

The political heritage: Suárez's role in the alternation of power

Having helped to mastermind the transition, Adolfo Suárez surely also facilitated the creation of a modern parliamentary democracy in Spain. Having abandoned the UCD, a party which was rapidly disappearing (it won just 7.3 per cent of the votes cast in the 1982 elections), he remained faithful to his centrist project. But his new party, the CDS, was never able to win more than the 10 per cent of votes it obtained in the European parliamentary and the municipal elections of 1987. The Spanish political system began to polarise between the socialists and the conservatives of the Allianza Popular. Taking his part in constructive opposition to the socialist government, Suárez continued to encourage the centrism of Spanish political life until his resignation from politics in 1991, following his party's defeat in that year's municipal elections. If this setback was due to confusing electoral tactics, incomprehensible to the voter since they were oriented both to the left and to the right, Suárez also contributed to the recentralisation of the Spanish right, now reincarnated as the Partido Popular, if only by leaving to it the necessary political space. Suárez acknowledged that his dream of offering an alternative to the hegemony of the Socialist Party had become an illusion. Thus it was that both before and after the general election of 1996 Suárez offered his good offices to both the young José Maria Aznar and Felipe González in order to be sure that the new alternation of power would take place without incident and without the faintest suspicion of *revanchisme*. As Suárez put it, 'political transitions are always in some way a form of transaction' (Suárez, 1996, p. 334).

Suárez withdrew definitively from Spanish politics in 1993, having even urged the dissolution of the CDS, and notwithstanding the temptations of a political comeback at the 1996 general election he resolutely devoted himself to his private life. He had fulfilled his tasks. Spain had been fully reintegrated into the international community (having been granted accession to NATO in 1982, just before the socialists came to power, and to the EEC in 1986, after the completion of negotiations initiated by his government). Spanish democracy had taken vigorous root and proved its hardiness with a full alternation of power. The Spanish economy had been consolidated, fundamental political confrontations mostly overcome and society liberalised. In 1996 Adolfo Suárez's political 'rehabilitation' finally began when he was awarded the Blanquerna Prize by Jordi Pujol, the new Catalan leader, for his contribution to the reconciliation of the Spanish people. This was followed by a number of prizes and awards to the 'Don', twenty years after he had first come to power. In December 1998, as this chapter was nearing completion, the *Economist* magazine ran a profile on Spanish Prime Minister Jose Maria Aznar. It described how Aznar had

> steadily swum towards the middle. Madrid's leftish intelligentsia have sniffed in vain for the ghost of General Franco lurking in Mr Aznar's boudoir. The rigid, right-wing Catholic moralists of Opus Dei have been hard to uncover at the heart of government. Spain's small band of economically liberal Thatcherites remain mostly on Mr Aznar's fringe.... Instead, Mr Aznar's own acolytes in his People's Party refer to themselves firmly as the 'centre-right', 'the reforming right' or even just 'centrist' – never, it seems, the plain, unqualified right (*The Economist*, 5 December 1998).

That centrist tendency on the right was further confirmed on 19 January 1999 when Aznar appointed Javier Arenas as party secretary (Arenas, who thus became Aznar's political heir, was a renowned centrist and former member of Suárez's defunct UCD party) and, one month later, at the twelfth congress of the Partido Popular, when he launched a rebranding of the party's politics as 'reformist centre'. This determined centrism on the right was Adolfo Suárez's true and perhaps most precious legacy to the modern Spanish democracy he created.

Adolfo Suárez: chronology

1932	Born in Cerebros (Ávila) to a well-to-do family. Suárez had to take care of his younger brother when his father, a republican sympathiser, left home to work in Madrid.
1950s, early	Member of Catholic Action. Founded the 'de Jovenes a Jovenes' student association.
1954	Finished law studies in Ávila and Salamanca.
1956–57	Head of the first section of the civic government of Ávila, a post in the gift of Fernando Herrero Tejedor, a man close both to Opus Dei and to the National Movement (former Phalangists).
1958	Head of cabinet of Herrero Tejedor, governor of Logrono.
1961	Head of the technical cabinet of Herrero Tejedor, Vice president of the National Movement.
1964	Nominated technical administrator at the Naval Social Institute and deputy head of public relations in the civil government.
1968	Civil governor of Segovia. Suárez's first government post.
1969	Director general of radio-diffusion and television.
1973	Chairman of the National Tourism Company.
1975	Deputy secretary general then minister for the National Movement.
1976	Appointed prime minister.
1981	Resigned as prime minister. Leopoldo Calvo Sotelo succeeded him and tried to obtain a majority. After a first attempt, the second vote in the Cortes was interrupted by the attempted *coup d'état* led by Lieutenant-Colonel Tejero.
1982	The PSOE won the legislative elections. Suárez quit the UCD and founded the CDS.
1991	Suárez quit the CDS following defeat in the municipal elections.

Notes

1 In this guise, Juan Carlos somewhat obscured Adolfo Suárez's brave role after the 1981 attempted *coup d'état* of Lieutenant-General Tejero. But, as the photograph reproduced in this volume graphically illustrates, it was Suárez, as outgoing prime minister, who courageously ran down the steps of the Cortes to help Deputy Prime Minister Gutiérrez Mellado, who was being physically assaulted by putschist members of the Guardia Civil. Indeed Suárez and Mellado, together with Santiago Carrillo, were the only parliamentarians to stay on their feet in defiance of the *coup*.

2 It is possible to discern broader and narrower definitions of the Spanish transition process. In a sense, Franco himself had sown the seeds of reform through his favouring of young Opus Dei technocrats in the 1950s, ultimately resulting in the economic reforms of the 1970s. Franco's death, the appointment of the Arias Navarro government in 1975 or of the Suárez government in 1976 all represent possible starting points under a more narrow definition. Similarly the holding of the 1977 elections, the adoption

of the 1978 constitution, the 1979 second legislative elections, Suárez's resignation in 1981 and Gonzalez's electoral victory in 1982 all represent possible ends of the process under a narrower definition. Under a broader definition the transition process was finally consolidated by the full alternation of power in the 1996 elections.

3 On the other hand Suárez did avoid consulting the 'mixed committee', jointly composed of the government and the (Francoist) senate, which could well have emasculated the law and would at least have slowed the reform process.

4 There was a general air of instability in the Mediterranean during this period, with political violence taking place in Turkey and the recent ousting of the colonels in Greece.

5 On the other hand it should be pointed out that, unlike the five other leaders of transition considered in this volume, Suárez was exceptional in that he actually won not one election but two.

References

Abella, Carlos (1997) *Adolfo Suárez* (Madrid: Espasa Calpe).

Clemente, Josep Carles (1994) *Historias de la transition 1973–1981* (Madrid: Editorial Fundamentos).

Hermet, Guy, (1986) *L'Espagne au XXe siècle* (Paris: Presses universitaires de France).

Preston, Paul (1986) *The Triumph of Democracy in Spain* (London: Routledge).

Preston, Paul (1995) *The Politics of Revenge: Fascism and the Military in 20th Century Spain* (London: Routledge).

Suárez, Adolfo (1995) *El Mundo, '7 dias'*, 23 July.

Suárez, Adolfo (1996) *Fue posible la concordia* (Madrid: Edición de Abel Hernández, Espasa Calpe).

7
Conclusions: Vision and Will

Martin Westlake

Where there is no vision, the people perish (*Proverbs*, 29.18)

An important consequence of political change is further, perhaps less predictable change, as all of the foregoing accounts have demonstrated. In this sense all the political leaders considered here were riding Mitterrand's metaphorical tiger (or to use F. W. de Klerk's equally graphic metaphor, riding their canoes through the rapids). They could not know exactly where the process of change might lead and, although they all had shrewd ideas about where the forces of opposition and reaction were to be found, they could not know how the balance of forces would pan out. Yet it is also clear that all these political leaders consciously launched a process of change, that each had a final objective in mind, and that each strove to bring about that objective. In other words, each displayed vision and will.

For Mikhail Gorbachev the vision was some sort of liberalising (by 1988, pluralistic) political and economic reform which would enable the USSR to modernise its creaking economic and social system. He could have had no idea of the enormity of the changes which would ultimately occur, but once that process of change was under way he adapted to it and continued to manage it through to its logical end. In contrast Adolfo Suárez's objective was clear from the outset: an ordered transition from the cabalistic oligarchy of the late Franco period to an orthodox Western-style democracy and market economy. Aided and abetted by King Juan Carlos, he displayed great political skill in making his vision a reality. In public F. W. de Klerk seemed to have been a late convert to the transition cause. In private, as Welsh and Spence show, de Klerk's misgivings about the apartheid system had gradually crystalised and, like Suárez, once he had fixed upon his

157

objective (again, an ordered transition) he refused to be diverted from it.

As becomes plain from John Fitzmaurice's analysis, Jaruzelski was hardly a consistent advocate of democracy, but he was always a patriot, and the common thread running through his actions in 1981 (martial law) and 1989 (lifting the ban on Solidarnosc) was his vision of a Polish solution to the problems raised by the growing political and social forces for change within the country. Just as the imposition of martial law may have staved off the threat of Soviet intervention, so the Magdelenka round table agreement avoided the menace of a decline into violent anarchy once the Soviet threat had disappeared.

Achille Occhetto's vision of a party transformed from permanent internal exile into a party of governance (thus assuring the transformation of the Italian political system from 'polarised pluralism' to full democracy) was clear from the beginning and never faltered, despite the vagaries of two fraught party conferences.

The day after his election as Labour Party leader, Neil Kinnock confided his reformist intentions to his deputy leader, Roy Hattersley, based on his vision of a centre-left party of mainstream opposition, able to be elected and willing to accept the responsibilities of government. Though buffetted by such events as the miners' strike and questioned by electoral defeat, Kinnock persisted with a reformist agenda which was ultimately to bear fruit in 1997.

Thus, vision and will are factors common to all the leaders considered here. But although these may be necessary qualities, they are hardly sufficient in themselves.

Luck, skill and judgement

Gorbachev, de Klerk, Jaruzelski, Suárez, Occhetto and Kinnock were all politically astute individuals, and it is clear that they would probably also have thrived in other political systems or circumstances. All were blessed with prodigious talent (all rose to lead their parties) and innate (though perhaps flawed) political skills, skills which had been honed in the course of their preceding, orthodox political careers. These leaders shared an acute but subtle political intelligence which enabled them to see the broader political canvas against which they were playing. Indeed it was perhaps these perceptive powers of political analysis which encouraged them to adopt the broader vision which, in turn, enabled them to see both the possibility and the necessity for change.

Napoleon famously favoured generals who had luck,[1] but his understanding of the term was particular: lucky generals were expected not only to make their luck but also to be able to exploit it. One could similarly argue that each of the leaders considered in this volume was 'lucky'. Gorbachev's rise to power was the result of happy circumstances, but he was also lucky to assume power at a time when, paradoxically, two crucial Western leaders who had modelled their political personas on the old Cold War style were nevertheless receptive to the idea of change. Ronald Reagan's 1986 Reykjavik agreement to mutual arms reductions demonstrated to Gorbachev that a genuine window of opportunity existed, should he choose to exploit it. He was further encouraged by Margaret Thatcher, who increasingly saw him as a rising star with whom the West might, to paraphrase her own words, be able to 'do business'. It was their orthodox Cold War stances which rendered Reagan and Thatcher reasonably immune to charges of having 'gone soft' on communism and enabled them to adopt encouraging approaches towards *glasnost* and *perestroika*. Gorbachev also proved fortunate later in his period of office in that he was able to negotiate with a great West German chancellor, Helmut Kohl, who was determined to consummate his leadership with the historical achievement of German unification and was therefore open to political and economic deal-making with the occupying powers. But it was Gorbachev who exploited these opportunities to such good effect.

Adolfo Suárez's greatest stroke of luck was undoubtedly being chosen by King Juan Carlos and receiving the benign support of the king thereafter. The monarchy had always kept its distance from the authoritarian regime, and hence the king's decision to opt for the hitherto orthodox Francoist technocrat was a huge advantage which doubtless helped propel Suárez along the path of historical destiny. Without the king's support, Suárez's widely criticised appointment as prime minister would almost certainly have led to ignominious failure and rapid replacement. With it, Suárez felt sufficiently confident to take the reform process to its conclusion. But if Suárez was initially dealt a good hand of cards, he nevertheless had to play them with great dexterity, and as Parlier shows, the strategy and tactics of the successful transition process were largely his.

In retrospect de Klerk enjoyed two important pieces of luck. The first was the topography of the political situation he inherited. On the one hand there were both the negative and the positive consequences of P. W. Botha's clumsy and aborted attempts at minimal political change. Botha's reforms may have been botched, but the sting of the principle of reform had already been drawn. On the other hand de Klerk had to deal with the National Party split and the creation of the Conservative Party. In his attempts to avoid haemorrhage de Klerk was obliged, perhaps inadvertently, to take up the reactionary stances which were to give him the political credibility to relaunch the transition process in a more radical way than Botha could ever have contemplated. F. W. de Klerk was also fortunate that Nelson Mandela had identified him (in a way reminiscent of the decision of Juan Carlos) as his preferred agent of change. As Welsh and Spence describe, the two thereafter developed an almost symbiotic relationship which survived a number of profound crises and ultimately led them both through to a successful, peaceful transition and a shared Nobel Peace Prize.

Jaruzelski's luck was also twofold. In the first place, by the late 1980s it had become apparent that Gorbachev's post-Afghanistan Soviet Union was much less likely to embark on further reactionary military interventions, even within the Warsaw Pact area. As Fitzmaurice makes clear, however, this was by no means a certainty, and in any case Gorbachev could have been replaced or overruled. Nevertheless Jaruzelski enjoyed far more room for manoeuvre than any previous Polish leader could have hoped for. In the second place, Jaruzelski was able to open negotiations in 1988 with a by now mature Solidarnosc leadership. Jaruzelski could argue that his actions in 1981 had in themselves chastened and matured Solidarnosc, but they could just as easily have provoked the opposite reaction.

Achille Occhetto similarly benefited from the consequences of Gorbachev's reforms, the collapse of the Soviet-backed regimes in Eastern Europe enabling him to argue forcefully that the PCI's remaining orthodox communist trappings risked rapidly becoming an irrelevance which would lead the party into a post-Cold War electoral *cul-de-sac* and inexorable decline.

Neil Kinnock was perhaps the exception that proved the rule. He had an extraordinary run of luck in his rise to the leadership, ranging from his selection to a Westminster seat at the age of 28, to Tony Benn's defeat at the 1983 general election (which left Kinnock as the Labour left's strongest contender for the leadership), to the party's adoption of a new mechanism for leadership elections. Thereafter – his friends would certainly argue – his luck appeared to run out. But as a convinced reformist inheriting a weak and divided party, Kinnock at least had the luck of being in opposition, enabling the party to settle its problems and heal its wounds without the distraction of government. Though Kinnock himself might never agree, some would argue that he was actually fortunate to lose the 1992 general election, thereby avoiding the debilitating experience of presiding over the run on the pound and the ignominious ejection of sterling from the ERM in October 1992. (Having always maintained that sterling had entered the ERM at an overambitious exchange rate, Kinnock would have immediately sought a realignment of parities after election. But even if this had proved sufficient to ward off the speculative intent of the markets, one of the earliest acts of Kinnock's premiership would hence have been to confirm Labour's reputation as a party of devaluation.)

Another quality common to all these leaders was judicious flexibility and the ability to adapt to the unfolding consequences of change. All were adept at the skilful manoeuvring so necessary to bring transition policy successfully across the divide. Similarly all displayed a strong streak of ruthlessness and determination: Gorbachev may have eschewed Stalinist methodology to rid himself of his political opponents but he did speedily replace the Politburo colleagues he inherited; Jaruzelski, although he has always denied direct responsibility, was at least morally implicated in the order for troops to open fire on anticommunist demonstrators, and he had been prepared to impose martial law; de Klerk showed a Kohl-like ability to see off potential rivals; and in their different ways Suárez, Occhetto and Kinnock all managed their parties with steely determination.

Another common characteristic of most of these political leaders was their ability to catch the forces of those opposed to change off balance by the radical and unexpected nature of their initiatives. Gorbachev's announcement of *glasnost* and *perestroika* came as a daring but calculated blow to the old Soviet military and political castes. Suárez's genius was to manoeuvre those same reactionary castes into opting for change themselves, but their choice of what they saw as the lesser of several evils was in itself conditioned by his unilateral triggering of the transition process. For Occhetto and Kinnock the element of surprise was also of crucial importance: both Occhetto's October 1989 announcement of his intention to reform the PCI and Kinnock's 1985 Bournemouth conference declaration of war on the Militant Tendency came as bolts out of the blue, momentarily stunning the potential opposition and allowing further advantage to be gained before more reactionary elements could rally themselves. F. W. de Klerk twice exploited the element of surprise, with his February 1990

Cape Town announcement lifting the ban on the ANC and again in risking all in the March 1992 referendum following the National Party's potentially disastrous loss in the Potchefstroom by-election. Of the six leaders considered in this volume, Jaruzelski was the least able to exploit the advantage of surprise, although he tried on at least three occasions: first with the imposition of martial law (the shock effects rapidly dwindled, particularly after Gorbachev came to power in the USSR); second with the 29 November 1988 referendum (which failed to win the necessary majority support of the electorate); and third through the February 1989 Magdalenka round table and his insistence on early elections (of which a suspicious Solidarnsoc was understandably fearful).

Courage and fortitude

All six leaders possessed an extraordinary degree of self-belief and displayed great courage, particularly when they sought to sieze the initiative at key moments. At the very least they laid their political careers on the line (and all ultimately paid the price). At the most, as the attempted *coups d'état* in the Soviet Union and Spain graphically illustrated, they put themselves at genuine physical risk (de Klerk, too, must surely at times have feared an assassin's bullet).

To these leaders' acts of undoubted political courage can be added considerable fortitude, as they hold to their views and strategies in the face of sustained and at times vicious attack. Naturally they would have known that such attacks were inevitable, given that their strategies necessarily involved the severe erosion of vested interests. But even if they were able to brace themselves in anticipation, they also had to display the precious soldierly attribute of steadfastness under fire.

Political alter egos

Three of the case studies revealed the existence of what might be termed political alter egos, that is, there existed someone or something to play off. Welsh and Spence point out how Nelson Mandela saw a strong de Klerk as being to his advantage and therefore sought to avoid undermining his position. Similarly, Fitzmaurice describes how General Jaruzelski both used and was used by Solidarnosc. Ironically in both these cases political alter egos proved ultimately to be political nemeses. Adolfo Suárez's alter ego was King Juan Carlos, who bestowed the historical legitimacy of the monarchy on the transition project.

Heads of state and heads of party

An important distinction must be made between the four leaders who were or became heads of state or government – Gorbachev, de Klerk, Jaruzelski and Suárez – and the two leaders who were heads of party alone – Occhetto and Kinnock. It could be argued that those who headed their states or governments enjoyed greater power and hence greater latitude. They could not control international factors (for example the American Star Wars initiative, or international sanctions or the threat of a Soviet invasion), but in domestic terms they called most of the shots. Those not in government were subject to a very different set of dynamics. Both Occhetto and Kinnock used the freedom which exclusion from governance gave them to try to bring an end to that same exclusion. In other words their aims were on a different scale, but that different scale also constrained their range of options.

The 'de Gaulle syndrome'

All the leaders considered in this study served orthodox political apprenticeships. Some may have won their political spurs as internal 'revolutionaries' (Kinnock refused to join the 1976–79 Callaghan government as a junior minister, Occhetto was 'exiled' to Sicily for his youthful left-wing views), but all proved that they could 'play the game' as team players. To put it another way, they were appointed because they seemed reassuringly orthodox. As Brown emphasises, Gorbachev was so adept at respecting the Soviet orthodoxies that few had any suspicion that he might harbour serious reformist intent. De Klerk was considered to be on the right of his party and was therefore a reassuring presence for the reactionary supporters of apartheid. Jaruzelski was an archetypal establishment figure of communist Poland – a pro-Soviet career soldier and faithful son of the *apparat*. Despite Suárez's anonymity, Juan Carlos was able to present him as at least a safe pair of Francoist hands. Occhetto had been Natta's right-hand man. Kinnock was a quintessential party man, well on the left.

Could they have carried through their reforms if they had not had this orthodoxy? The answer, almost certainly, is that they could not. Gorbachev, for example, secretly believed in a paradox: the Soviet system could only be changed from the top, yet only orthodox servants of the system could rise to the top. 'Aliens' were normally identified and seen off by the system long before they got their hands on the levers of central power. Indeed one of Gorbachev's most extraordinary achievements was to dupe the system for so long without succumbing to the orthodoxies he was obliged to reiterate so frequently.

F. W. de Klerk has consistently denied that he was a 'reactionary' (*verkrampt*) but he admits that this was the way he was perceived and, implicitly, the impression he wanted to give. The reason was simple: had he been perceived as being less reactionary his National Party would surely have suffered a severe loss of supporters to Treurnicht's breakaway Conservative Party and other political extremes. As Nelson Mandela recognised in his autobiography, the existence of such a profound division on the white right wing – between radicals and moderates – would have made a peaceful transition impossible.

It is similarly impossible to imagine the peaceful transition which ultimately occurred in Poland without the figure – afterwards so widely loathed ! – of General Jaruzelski. A civilian politician would not have enjoyed the instinctive support of the military establishment. Jaruzelski's conservative credentials – both for reactionaries at home and in the Soviet Union – were confirmed by his past actions, and in particular the fact that he had been morally complicit in ordering troops to fire on demonstrators and had imposed martial law. For those who feared change, Jaruzelski must have seemed reassuringly authoritarian. He certainly seemed to sport repressive instincts which must have been reassuring to the top brass of the Polish Communist Party and the Polish army.

As already described, Adolfo Suárez's appointment was criticised by the right for every reason bar one – he was undeniably, and reassuringly, a creature of the Francoist system. Achille Occhetto and Neil Kinnock were similarly orthodox creatures of their parties.

Gorbachev's observed paradox could be dubbed the 'de Gaulle syndrome'; who, other than General de Gaulle, could have extricated France from Algeria without revolution and major bloodshed? In fact the 'de Gaulle syndrome' is a broadly observable political phenomenon. The reformists (as opposed to revolutionaries) most likely to succeed are those who come from the heart of the system they wish to reform, as the six case studies in this volume make amply clear.

Motivation

We turn at last to the key question of motivation – what made them embark on a process of change? After all, as the Introduction observed, for all those studied here the easiest or the most obvious solution would have been to opt for some variation of the *status quo*, with its implication of decadence and gradual deterioration. But some inner conviction, combined with personal courage and acute powers of political analysis, led them to choose a far more radical path.

A hint of their motivation can be gleaned from the way in which all subsequently described their strategies in terms of personal responsibility. The contributions to this volume provide intense and harrowing quotations from, variously, de Klerk, Jaruzelski, Suárez and Kinnock in which each insisted on taking personal responsibility for what had occurred – both the positive and the negative. Politicians are notorious for retrospective self-justification, but there is more to it than that. Each believed or came to believe that they were part of a larger process which went beyond normal politicking; in other words they saw themselves as part of an ethical process.

Similar impressions can be gleaned from three other common themes. The first is the high level of self-belief they displayed, even going beyond the parameters of the system within which they had so far existed and operated. It is impossible to know the origin of such self-belief, but all these leaders, with the partial and ambiguous exception of Gorbachev (his father was an orthodox communist and his mother a religious believer), shared another common experience: a strong ethical upbringing in childhood and youth. In de Klerk's case the idiosyncratic values of the small *Dopper* church were carried over into adulthood and complemented by the high morality of the *Broederbond*. Jaruzelski experienced an orthodox and devout Catholic education, and on to this was successively grafted Russian communism and patriotic Polish militarism. Suárez was brought up in the strict mores of Spanish Catholicism before sinking into the bigotry of the Francoist technocracy. Occhetto was similarly given a traditional Catholic upbringing before plunging – in classic postwar Italian fashion – into the disciplined neotheocracy of Togliatti's Communist Party. Neil Kinnock was brought up in the bible-respecting Welsh valleys (his oratory remains infused with biblical allusions to this day). To this classic mixture of Christianity and socialism was added the formative experience of accompanying his mother, a district nurse, on her rounds to the poor, the afflicted and the dispossessed.

Thus all these leaders had a solid ethical grounding. The exception in Gorbachev's case is interesting. His first twenty-two years were lived in the repressive atmosphere of Stalin's Soviet Union. But as Gorbachev himself was later to describe, radically reformist ideas gradually grew within him, fuelled by reading and travel – privileges reserved for the trusted and the politically orthodox.[2]

A strong religious upbringing is not in itself an explanatory factor. The ogre Stalin studied in an Orthodox Church seminary and there are countless, less extreme examples of the opposite tendency. Nevertheless religion, with its recognition of alternative spiritual power bases (Rome in particular) and ethical systems, may have given the leaders discussed in this book the conceptual ability to imagine systems other than those in which they had so far functioned, particularly when allied to an ethical dimension.

A second important common factor was these leaders' eschewal of repressive and/or unorthodox methods that would go beyond the reasonable use of power. Nobody knew better than Mikhail Gorbachev how the Soviet state's mechanism could be used to crush opposition, but as power slipped away from the Soviet Communist Party he refused to declare the state of emergency which both colleagues and enemies urged upon him. A large network of men of violence apparently overlapping the apparatus of the South African state impatiently awaited the call from F. W. de Klerk – a call which, pointedly, never came. General Jaruzelski *did* impose martial law in 1981, but he never seriously considered a repressive response in 1988/89. Neil Kinnock remained resolutely committed to parliamentary democracy, and because of this determination to win through the ballot box he sternly eschewed calls from the far left for extra-parliamentary struggle during the long years of Margaret Thatcher's successive administrations. Most notably, perhaps, Adolfo Suárez's great *coup* was to get the Francoists to vote for change; not quite the equivalent of turkeys voting for Christmas, but certainly for the end of the regime which had guaranteed them patronage. Only Achille Occhetto appears to have deviated from this trend. His decision to announce the dissolution of the PCI unilaterally rather than work his proposal through the party's democratic machinery was a tactical *fait accompli*, but it led to a painful internal commotion which might perhaps have been avoided if the leader had opted for more traditional methods.

A sceptic would argue that there could have been good cynical reasons for these leaders to act as they did. With their positions of autocratic power already eroded by their changing circumstances,

Mikhail Gorbachev and General Jaruzelski may have sensed that they might one day have to answer for their actions. F. W. de Klerk may have had similar intimations. Adolfo Suárez wanted to remain in power after the transition. At the least, if these four leaders saw transition as inevitable, they might have been trying to manage a soft landing for themselves and the interests for which they stood. Achille Occhetto and Neil Kinnock wanted to become prime minister of their respective countries. And all these leaders must have had a weather eye on posterity.

But there are also more noble potential explanations. In particular the scruples that led them to introduce change in the first place would have later denied them more autocratic means of blocking opposition within the system. Moreover, if they led changes towards democracy, or towards more democratic regimes, it may also have been because they believed (or came to believe) in such a conceptual alternative, with all of its implications for their own actions.

A third common factor can be seen in the fact that all these leaders saw power as a means rather than an end. Many modern-day governments seem more attached to management than to manifesto commitments, and some only formulate their policies after they have been elected. But each of these leaders had an 'agenda' – they wanted power because they wanted to do things with it.

None of the common factors identified in this chapter – a strong sense of historical destiny and personal responsibility, self-belief, courage, fortitude, vision, will, luck, skill, judgement, a moral/ethical dimension, the eschewal of repressive tactics, a vision of power primarily as a means – of themselves have any explanatory value, but it is the particular combination of these factors which may be significant. Andrei Grachev's wonderful description of Mikhail Gorbachev as 'a genetic error in the system' touches on the nub of the phenomenon. All the leaders considered here were the intimate fruit of the systems they changed, and yet they were somehow able to raise their vision, step outside the system, and identify how and why it should be changed.

Another theme common to all the leaders studied in this volume is the relative importance they gave to values and the way in which they were able to shrug off ideological restraints. Each made a personal journey away from a previous ideological orthodoxy – Gorbachev from communism, de Klerk from apartheid, Jaruzelski from Soviet communism, Suárez from Francoism (if that can be termed an ideology), Occhetto from Euro-communism and Kinnock from left-wing socialism – but did not discover another. As has been speculated in relation to the case of Neil Kinnock, the way in which they were able to break out of previous ideological restraints (none of them were ever tempted to return to the 'bunker') almost certainly facilitated their roles as leaders of transition, but so too, probably, did their lack of strong attachment to any alternative ideology. In this respect they were almost certainly reflecting a more general trend away from a strong ideological emphasis, particularly after the end of the Cold War (or in Suárez's case during the earlier thaw represented by the development of Euro-communism) and the collapse of all the 'certainties' that had engendered. These individuals therefore probably represented a new trend towards managerial, technocratic, unideological political leadership in an unideological age.

Transition as process

Transition is a process, enacted over time, and it is useful to distinguish between at least three different stages, and hence leaders' roles during each of them. It is beyond dispute that each of the leaders under consideration in this study *initiated* the process of change (no sign of Mitterrand's tiger yet!), and the authors of the case studies attempt to provide explanations of why they acted in such a way.

There then follows the transition period itself. Having initiated the process, the leaders attempted to guide or control it, presumably towards some predetermined destination. The extent to which they were so able to guide and control varied (here the tiger was at its most forceful, perhaps), as did the degree to which their preferred destination was formulated. For example, as Brown relates, Mikhail Gorbachev wanted to introduce reform into the Soviet system, but he certainly did not intend at the outset to turn the Soviet Union into a pluralist democracy and at no point did he wish to see the break-up of the USSR. In contrast Adolfo Suárez always intended to lead the process of transition towards a modern democratic state. However well-formulated their preferred end-state, the six leaders showed similar traits in managing the second stage of transition, and these have been considered at some length in this chapter.

In the end, there is the third and final stage of the transition process: consolidation. Here these leaders' visions failed in one important sense for, with the possible exception of F. W. de Klerk and General Jaruzelski, none of them envisaged a future in which they did not figure. Yet ironically, that, is what occurred in each and every case. In part this irony must be due to their own actions. As Martin Bull points out, 'the very changes generated can undermine the leader's power base, and the benefits of transition may not come immediately. Consequently, as the transition phase begins to close it can take its leader with it.' In that context all the leaders considered in this volume share another characteristic: they are all either villified in their own countries or have been forgotten:

> Resented by the era from which they form a bridge and discounted by that in which they establish the bridgehead, they are seen by the old guard as heresy and by the avant garde as embarrassment. Yet they led the way. They showed courage while courage was still needed. They looked into the unknown. With hindsight their vision seems incomplete, over-cautious. The first forays into new thinking usually do. But what vision it was at the time! (Parris, 1997).

It was a phenomenon Nicolo Machiavelli had identified almost 500 years before:

> It must be considered that there is nothing more difficult to carry out, nor more doubtful of success, nor more dangerous to handle, than to initiate a new order of things. For the reformer has enemies in all those who profit by the old order, and only lukewarm defenders in all those who would profit by the new order (Machiavelli, 1952, pp. 49–50).

Inevitable demise?

Was there a common explanatory factor in the demise of these six leaders? As we have seen, they achieved their objectives to a greater or lesser extent but paradoxically found themselves marginalised in the process. Why? Why did these consummate politicians seem unable to hold on to power? These six case studies appear to have identified a number of potential explanatory factors.

A first is timing. The benefits of transition are not immediately apparent and there is often pain to go through first – particularly for the old vested interests. Consequently the benefits of transition may well become apparent too late for the leader of transition to benefit from them himself. Rather it is his successors who reap the rewards (for example Yeltsin in the case of Gorbachev, Walesa in the case of Jaruzelski, González in the case of Suárez, Prodi and D'Alema in the case of Occhetto, Blair in the case of Kinnock). The leader of transition, meanwhile, is more likely to be associated with the pain.

In the second place, leaders of transition are necessarily associated with a particular phase of the regime. In part this must be because of the 'de Gaulle syndrome' described above: these leaders came from the heart of the establishment. But perhaps they are associated to such an extent that it is felt that the completion of the transition process and the emergence of a genuinely new regime necessarily involves going beyond the leader of the transition himself. In order for the transition to be consummated, the leaders of transition must be rejected and abandoned. After all they are tainted by their provenance from the old world and are therefore unsuited to take the regime into the brave new world. If this is true, then the great irony is that their demise would appear to have been an inevitable part of the transition process which they themselves initiated.

Conclusions

From the analyses set out in this book, it seems clear that all these leaders acted with reference to a set of higher moral values – be it patriotism, loyalty or commitment to parliamentary democracy. This ethical framework – wherever it came from – formed an important part of their overall vision, and it made them not only ethical beings but also, in a sense, ethical actors. The democratisation of Russia, Poland, Spain and South Africa, a social-democratic coalition government in Italy, new Labour in power in the United Kingdom – as John Fitzmaurice reminds us, it is easy to be wise after the event and with 20:20 vision, but none of the above were foregone conclusions. Spain and South Africa could so easily have collapsed into bloody civil war. The Soviet Union was generally deemed to be impervious to reform and Russia and Poland could have collapsed into anarchic chaos. Through the absence of plausible opposition, Italy and the United Kingdom might have been condemned to many more years of rule by party oligarchies. Even if one discounts the probability of anarchy and chaos, other alternatives were on offer. As Brown points out in his chapter, 'economic failure and inflexibly oppressive regimes are very common throughout the world'. All the leaders considered in this volume might never have been, and all might have failed. Therefore, we should perhaps be grateful for these leaders of transition and for the felicitous historical accidents that threw up such individuals at such moments and gave them the chance to succeed.

Notes

1 'Has he luck?' Perhaps apocryphal, but cited in *The Oxford Dictionary of Quotations* (Oxford: Oxford University Press, 1985).
2 Perhaps also of significance was the fact that both of Gorbachev's grandfathers had been arrested on trumped-up political charges during Stalin's assault on the peasantry in the 1930s (Brown, 1996, p. 25).

References

Brown, Archie (1996) *The Gorbachev Factor* (Oxford: Oxford University Press).
De Klerk, F. W. (1999) *The Last Trek: A New Beginning* (London: Macmillan).
Fukuyama, Francis (1992) *The End of History and the Last Man* (London: Hamilton)
Machiavelli, Niccolo (1952) *The Prince* (London: New English Library).
Parris, Matthew (1997) 'Heroes of Transition', *The Times*, 7 March.

Index